Footprints on the Track

FOOTPRINTS ON THE TRACK

Anglo-Indian Railway Memories

Edited by
NOEL THOMAS

Anglo-Ink

First Published in 2013

Second Edition 2014

This book is funded by **The Philip Lawrence Wood Foundation**

Published by **Anglo-Ink**
A-77, 2nd Floor, 3rd Avenue, Anna Nagar East,
Chennai - 600 102, India.
Phone: +91 44 4208 0058 E-mail: angloink@gmail.com

Designed by
Harry MacLure Design Studio, Chennai, India.
Mobile: +91 98413 97502 E-mail: harrymaclure@yahoo.com

Printed at
Pio Printers Private Limited,
83, East Mada Church Road, Royapuram, Chennai, India.

Cover Photograph Courtesy: **Noel 'Bully' Netto**
Frontispiece art: **Samba**
Illustrations in the book: **Harry MacLure & Rebecca Taylor**

ISBN: 978-81-928188-0-1

To my grandchildren
Jordan, Aaron, Zara, Nathan and Eva

ACKNOWLEDGEMENTS

Louis de Cruze, Clifford and Brenda Smith
CSSAI - Toronto

Eugene D'Cruz - Sydney

Ron and Patricia Forbes - Toronto

Shane Calvert - Calcutta

Rebecca Taylor - Bangalore

Harry MacLure,
Sivaraj D. and Reuben Quental
of *Anglos In The Wind* - Chennai

CONTENTS

Foreword

For a child raised within sight and sound of trains and tracks, life was a schedule of arrivals and departures. The happiest arrival was Dad coming home from line, Mum applying her finishing touch to the lunch or dinner, we children rushing out to greet him, followed by our four dogs wagging their tails furiously. I followed in Dad's footsteps for forty-two years, so did five of my brothers for some time; so yes, I live with many railway memories, cherish and cling to them.

A young girl told me that an article I wrote in the 'Nostalgic' issue of *Anglos In The Wind* was a lovely fairytale. I understood why...Santa Claus coming riding on an elephant – incredible! Had I not seen it myself, true to my surname, I would never have believed it. But, I am not spinning yarns. As ninety-two year old Eugene D'Cruz puts it, "That's just the way it was!"

The little girl's comments made me put the brakes on for a while, until Margaret Deefholts had something nice to write about my railway reminiscences, as did Rudy Otter more recently. Margaret and Rudy are in a bigger league, so it needed no more urging from Harry MacLure for me to put all these memories together.

Yes, I saw those footprints on the track, albeit metaphorically. I was sixteen when Mack Johannes made the ultimate sacrifice, a nineteen year old railway apprentice when Percy Carroll made his heroic final run. I have crossed the famous James Bridge in Bilaspur division.

I was privileged to have worked under Mr. V. Anand who called Anglo-Indians "unsung heroes of the Indian Railways".

On a different note, I have, both as child and adult, enjoyed many a Christmas week and other functions in that spirit of pure entertainment that only a railway institute could provide. I have seen great feats of sportsmanship on our own railway grounds. Anglo-Indian railway life was not all blood, sweat and tears. It was also about sport, song and dance, fun and laughter.

Call it enigmatic if you like, but many like me were poor yet happy, happy with the bare necessities; basic requirements were full and plenty. We called it our Grandfather's Railway. It was the great provider. We loved it and gave it our all. The way we lived is worth recording for posterity and this book tries to do just that.

Much as we tried, we couldn't include some railway colonies viz. Adra, Bilaspur, Jubbalpore, Jhansi, Waltair, Nagpur, Agra, Lucknow, Hubli and many more. The reader may find some passing references to them. Perhaps, we could be more inclusive in a second edition, if there is someone left to tell the tale and send it to us.

Read this one first and I hope you enjoy it.

– Noel Thomas

In Frank Anthony's Words

Incomparable Railwaymen

The Indian Railways have been built literally on the blood and bones of the Anglo-Indian community. In times of the greatest stress, whether in war or during the most convulsive strikes, the Anglo-Indians have kept the wheels of India's life and economy moving. The same traditions have been continued in Independent India. During the several strikes since Independence, the Railways have been kept working because of the loyalty and courage of the Anglo-Indian railwaymen.

Civilian Services

But for the ready and complete response of the Anglo-Indian railwaymen, the Indian Railways could never have stood up to the unprecedented strain suddenly imposed by a vast and unexpected war effort. Long before 1939, those conversant with railway conditions had warned the Government that owing to the outworn and inadequate rolling stock the railways would collapse under the impact of war conditions. Only those who actually ran the trains could speak adequately of the almost superhuman effort that was required to keep them, and consequently the war effort, moving in India. The Railways were literally the wheels on which India's magnificent contribution to the war, in men and material, moved. This crucial service was only made possible by running staff having to work, very often, for unbroken periods of 20 to 30 hours at a time. The disturbances of August, 1942, made the position critical. Murder, arson and the uprooting of railway track were the order of the day. In the areas around Bihar and through which the troops and supplies, necessary to resist the Japanese invasion, had to be carried, conditions were chronic. But for the Anglo-Indian railwaymen and also for their military service in doing patrol and sentry duty, as members of the Auxiliary Force, the war effort would have been completely paralysed for a considerable period.

THE RAILWAYS

After the middle of the 19th century, the Anglo-Indians along with pioneering Britons laid the first railway sleepers in India. These Anglo-Indian pioneers were scattered all over the country. They lived under the most difficult conditions, having to hack their way through jungle and swamp and without any medical, much less social amenities. They were, usually, separated from their families for a period of 4 to 5 years. Because of the inhospitable, dangerous conditions under which work had to be done in those pioneering days up to 1920, members of the other communities were not forthcoming except for the lowest categories. With over a hundred years' intimate association with the building and working of the Railways, Anglo-Indians developed an almost hereditary aptitude for Railway Service.

Up till about 1920, practically every engine-driver, guard, station master and permanent way inspector was an Anglo-Indian or a Domiciled or Covenanted European. Anglo-Indians, usually of the fairer variety, reached the positions of Agents, now known as General Managers, Chief Engineers and General Traffic Managers. In order to break through the British wall of colour discrimination they had to masquerade as Europeans or at least as Domiciled Europeans.

The stability and progress of the Railways depended on the Anglo- Indians. Strikes were short-lived because of the sense of duty not only of the Anglo-Indian railwaymen but of their families. Thus, in 1923, there was a major strike on the then Eastern Railway when even the Anglo-Indian schoolboys came to the rescue of the Administration and cleaned railway carriages. In 1927, the then Bengal-Nagpur Railway was faced with a serious strike. Once again, the Anglo-Indian Community kept the wheels moving and prevented the strike from spreading to the other Railways. In 1928 there was another strike on the East Indian Railway when the Anglo-Indian railwaymen served beyond the call of duty in order to keep the goods and passenger trains moving.

In their private moments even the most ardent advocates of the egalitarian principle will admit that with the decline in the employment of Anglo-Indians, the sense of discipline and service in this great public utility concern has steadily and even precipitately fallen. Even today, the Anglo-Indian railwaymen are among the comparatively few who can be relied upon to do their duty and, indeed, more than their duty and not to hold the country to ransom by going on strike at the drop of a cap by some irresponsible trade union or would-be trade union leader.

The Railway Institute

Anglo-Indian Railway Institutes occupy a special niche in the Anglo-Indian social scheme. The Senior Institute, the 'Inster' as it was called, was usually the preserve of the Community especially where they were employed in large numbers. These Institutes were to be found right down the line on every railway. The Institutes were usually well-off financially and provided plenty of social amenities including tennis, billiards and, of course, regular dances. For the upper subordinates including the Class II and some Class I officers who had risen from subordinate positions, and the Class III staff from station masters and loco foremen down to guards and firemen – these Institutes were the centres of their social life.

Many of these Institutes were household names in the Community, such as the Burt Institute, Lahore, the Ajmer Institute, the Kharagpur Institute and a score of others. They usually had a very fine boarded dance floor, an excellent bar and at least one super band. The amenities, including tennis, billiards and swimming were as good as those in some of the 'burra' clubs.

Anglo-Indian railwaymen were in the front rank of sport in the country. Because of the opportunities at the Institutes they produced some of the finest tennis and billiard players in the Country.

The social functions at an Institute, especially the dances, were marked by a warmth and sense of fun that characterise the Community. The smallest Railway Institute could produce a string band as good as some of the finest professional bands.

It is not surprising that with so much musical talent we find, today, Anglo-Indians among the top pop singers in the world. To mention a few – Cliff Richard (formerly Harry Webb) of Lucknow, Tony Brent (formerly Reginald Bretagne) of Deolali, Engelbert Humperdinck (formerly Gerald Dorsey) of Madras, Eden Kane the son of Bert Sarstedt who was a senior Anglo-Indian official on the railway.

Excerpts from the book 'Britain's Betrayal in India'

Frank Anthony was an iconic Anglo-Indian leader and the first Anglo-Indian Member of Parliament of India

The Pioneers

Reginald Maher

The Anglo-Indian community can point with justifiable pride to its share in the building of the Indian Railways. The task of building a railway, though difficult in Britain, was nothing compared to the herculean effort required in India. In his History of the East Indian Railway, Huddleston writes:

"Beside the magnitude of the work, the construction of a railway was a novelty in India and a practical knowledge of the country, the people and their language had to be acquired.

About this time England was beset with troubles of her own, due to the Crimean War. Sufficient numbers of Englishmen were not forthcoming to set about the task of building a railway. The Anglo-Indian supplied a ready substitute. He knew the country, he had been born and bred in it; he knew the people; he conversed with them in their own languages. The supervisors and layers of the track were Anglo-Indians – a fact amply borne out by the virtual monopoly by Anglo-Indians of the posts of Permanent Way Officers before 1947."

It might not be irrelevant to introduce here an echo of this great building in distant Kenya forty years later. For the first Railway in that country was also built for the British by an

Anglo-Indian with labour from India. That no Englishman volunteered for the task may have been due to the fact that the project itself was not very favourably looked upon in Britain itself, where a London newspaper dubbed it "a lunatic line". The Anglo-Indian, R.O. Preston of Madras and his three hundred Punjabi mazadoors were pressed into service because Africans refused to do the work.

Excerpt from the book 'These are the Anglo-Indians'

This article was first published in The National Anglo-Indian Railway Convention Souvenir 2003, edited by Dr. Beatrix D'Souza, with the kind permission of Gordon Maher

UNSUNG HEROES OF THE RAILWAYS IN INDIA

V. Anand

A retired General Manager of Southern Railway, the author pays tribute to members of the Anglo-Indian community whose contribution was immense in making train services punctual and safe.

THE ANGLO-INDIANS undoubtedly made the Indian Railways what it is now. Their contribution to the development of the Indian Railways was immense. They dominated the supervisory and higher management echelons particularly in pre-Independence days.

Their most visible presence was in train operations and particularly the locomotive foot plate. Their least visible - almost invisible – but extremely important presence was in the telephone exchanges as Telephone Operators and in the Cipher Department.

The skills of Anglo-Indian locomotive drivers were legendary. Their pride in workmanship and their devotion to duty was unparalleled.

As I complete 40 years of association with Indian Railways, I recollect the fond memories of my foot plate training. While I can recall a few names who were veritable heroes on the foot plate, there were hundreds of such unsung heroes toiling 365 days in the year and 24 hours a day to make railway travel safe and punctual.

L to R: Driver Joe Selvey (hat under arm) and Fuel Inspector Jim Streeter. On Running Board: L to R: Firemen Vivian Magee and Eric Tenant

Photo Courtesy: Noel 'Bully' Netto

Every small boy of my generation has dreamt of being an engine driver. I was no exception. During my school days in Simla, I would run off to the railway station and peer through the boiler-tube fencing which separated the road from the railway tracks and watch the arrival and departure of the trains and the shunting movements. Occasionally, I was emboldened to run down from the booking office to the platform where I would land with a thump on the huge 'Avery' platform scale. My friends and I would take turns to jump on the platform scale to see who could register the maximum weight on the dial. We were, of course, chased away promptly by the station staff but we were undeterred till one day an engine driver stepped out and threatened to shove us into the firebox of the locomotive.

I used to gaze into the foot plate and admire the gleaming brass fittings and polished gauges. The engine driver in his immaculate navy blue woolen jacket would look down disdainfully. I resolved that one day I would enter the locomotive as a matter of right.

My first encounter with the Anglo-Indian running staff was at Asansol in Eastern Railway. In its heyday, the Asansol Steam Shed rivalled Bhusaval in Central Railway as the biggest Steam Shed. However, by the time we joined for training, the trunk routes had been electrified and our training was primarily on diesel and electric locomotives. Our Instructor was one Mr. Beale who used to play the saxophone at a local restaurant – an example of the versatility of the Anglo-Indian community. Mr. Rose was a Driving Instructor and he taught us the rudiments of electric locomotive running and maintenance. Though officially we were not allowed to drive, we were encouraged to do so by the Instructors under their watchful eye. It was only then that we learnt how much of skill is required to maintain punctual running.

The legendary drivers of Eastern Railway were, no doubt, Mr. Craker and Mr.Toker who used to work the diesel-hauled Mail trains. When the Rajdhani Express was introduced in 1969, I understand Mr. Craker took out the first train. Their knowledge of the route was profound. Mr. Craker could literally drive blind-folded, as he knew every feature of the track. I still remember telling him while on the foot plate of 5 Up Howrah - Amritsar Mail. "... Mr. Craker, you have just run through an ash pit at 100 kmph. Did you not know there is a speed restriction of 30 kmph! It says so right here in the Working Time Table!..."

Craker replied: "... Sir, the ash pit has been closed recently but the time table will be corrected only in the next issue. Till then, why should I slow down my train?"

Every shed had its own unofficial "speed king" - a driver who could be relied upon to coax that little extra out of the locomotive and run the trains punctually using every trick of the trade. Coincidentally they also had the best safety record and could judge the speed of the train without looking at a speedometer. (In any case, very few locomotives had speedometers in those days!).

After my training in Eastern Railway, I was sent for training to Southern Railway. However, it would not be out of place to ention Driver Ernest Dennison of South Eastern Railway who used to work the diesel locomotives of Waltair Shed attached to the 3 Up/4 Down Howrah-Chennai Mails. The first thing Dennison would do on entering the foot plate was to cross himself, take out the little crucifix which he had round his neck and hang it on the engine brake handle. It is said that when Dennison was the driver, 3 Up/4 Down Mail would never lose time.

The Erode Loco Shed, whether in its heyday of steam or in its present reincarnation as Diesel/Electric Loco Shed, is amongst the best on the Indian Railways. The quality of workmanship of the maintenance and the driving skills of the crew are unsurpassed. The steam engines, particularly those that went into Madras Railway, were treated with loving care. There was, however, a practical monetary aspect as the South Indian Railway (SIR) was liable to bear a heavy fine, if their loco failed on the Madras and Southern Maratha Railways (M&SM).

The speed king of Arakkonam Shed was Mr. Tennant. There was another famous driver by name Mr. Eugene D'Cruz who taught me the rudiments of steam loco driving and firemanship.

Our MG Loco Shed training was at Villupuram, where Mr. Andrew Batty used to take the 137 Down Trivandrum Express from Villupuram towards Madurai. The 180 kms of Villupuram-Tiruchirappalli section would be covered in 3 hours flat with one halt for watering at Vriddhachalam. By the time the train reached Lalgudi, the tender used to be almost empty. The drivers of Villupuram considered it "infra dig" to take water at Lalgudi. They would leave the village women disappointed as the water columns used to be made operative for 137 Down, but it would zoom pass without stopping. Mr. Andrew Batty's knowledge of the road was also immense and he considered that restricting the speed of the YP locomotives to 75 kmph was an insult to the excellent track and would, therefore, sometimes touch speeds up to 85 kmph with perfect safety.

Mr. Andrew Batty had a border-line case of cataract but such was the confidence of the Divisional Mechanical Engineer in Mr. Batty's safe driving that he was allowed to continue as an "A" Grade driver till his retirement and did not have to face the indignity of being medically decategorised.

Then there was the Besterwich family of which the driver from Madurai is remembered with admiration. When the firemen went on strike in 1968, Besterwich used to bring the train up to Tiruchirappalli with only one Yard Khalasi who had been given a crash course in firemenship. No train in his charge would lose time during a firemens' strike or otherwise. My interaction with drivers of Central Railway was at New Katni in Central Railway where the Dick brothers and Bent held sway. Stewart apart from being a good driver had great skills in diesel locomotive troubleshooting.

On one occasion an Anglo-Indian driver had written in the engine repair book ".... Engine failed due to thick black smoke white in colour coming out of exhaust ..." As we could not make anything out of the remark, we called the driver to the Shed and cranked the engine in his presence. When we asked him what he meant by "thick black smoke white in colour", he replied, "Sir, it is like Indira Gandhi's hair!" When the engine was cranked, we indeed found thick black smoke coming out of the exhaust with white plumes of steam. The turbo super charger casing had a crack with the result that it was not able to send enough air to the engine. This led to the "thick black smoke". The water was leaking out of the crack and getting converted into steam. With his choice of vocabulary, this driver had saved us hours of investigation.

From Katni, it was on to Bhusaval where the huge Steam Loco Shed was on the verge of closure. The Anglo-Indian drivers had progressed from steam to diesel and from diesel to electric locomotives. The most famous driver was Mr. Misquitta who could be relied upon to bring the train on time and was the inevitable choice for ceremonial special trains such as GM's Inspection.

Mr. Mascarenhas and Mr. Domingo were other names I can remember. The senior drivers had gone on to become supervisors and power controllers.

The two incidents I narrate now sum up the essence of Anglo-Indian engine drivers.

In those days, the Brindavan Express was perhaps the fastest train on the Indian Railways and I remember driver Vivian Magee (there was a write up about him in the popular Tamil Weekly "Ananda Vikadan") once covered the distance of 140 Kms. from Jolarpettai to Bangalore Cantonment in 1 hour and 40 minutes. The Brindavan Express was known for its punctuality and travelers waiting at Madras Central could set their watch at 19:45 hrs. by the arrival of 40 Up Brindavan Express. One day the train was 5 minutes late. The Chief Operating Superintendent (COPS) Mr. Godfrey Saldhana and Mr. E.S. Muthukrishnan, Chief Mechanical Engineer happened to be on the platform. When the train came to a halt, the COPS walked up to the engine and the following conversation ensued:

COPS : "... Magee! you are late!"

Magee : "So would you be, Sir, if you had to pass loop lines at five stations between Arakkonam and Madras."

Suffice it to say that the COPS called for the control charts and other records next day and ensured that the Brindavan Express would be given a line clear right through the main line. Such was his faith in Express drivers of the calibre of Magee.

Reginald D'Monte was a legend of Erode Loco Shed. On one occasion when he was driving 6 Up Nilgiri Express which was running a few minutes late, he received a message from Section Controller.

"... Driver of 6 Up to run at maximum permissible speed and make up time.."

Mr. D'Monte, however, did not make up a single minute. When he was called up by the Assistant Mechanical Engineer, Olavakkod to explain, he replied: "... Sir, does D'Monte have to be told to make up time?"

It is understood that the Assistant Mechanical Engineer issued orders that Section Controllers should not issue such messages which would hurt the pride of our mail engine drivers. For D'Monte safety and punctuality were articles of faith. The same D'Monte while driving 1 Down Mangalore Express, which started late, nearly an hour late from Madras, actually overtook Cochin Mail which had gone ahead.

One day a message was received that D'Monte was feeling unwell and complaining of chest pain and that a Doctor and ambulance should be ready at Erode. D'Monte ended his last trip with his hand still on the brake lever, by sheer will power. The moment he stepped out of the footplate he collapsed and was declared dead on arrival at the hospital. He was a true railwayman till his last breath.

Let us bow our heads to unsung heroes like D'Monte and send a prayer for their souls. Let us not forget our sacred duty to the travelling public. If we do so, the sacrifices made by railwaymen like D'Monte would have been in vain.

Editor's Note: Reginald D'Monte died at the age of 54 (born: 25th October 1916 – died: 30th December 1970)

This article was first published in The National Anglo-Indian Railway Convention Souvenir 2003, edited by Dr. Beatrix D'Souza

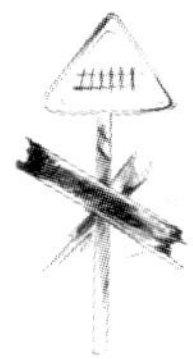

Railway Life In Anglo-India

Margaret Deefholts

Although many things have changed in modern India, Britain's legacy to the country in terms of institutions such as a parliamentary form of democracy, the judicial system, the civil service, the postal infrastructure and last, but far from least, the Indian Railways, have endured for over half a century.

Up to the time of India's Independence, the Railways offered the Anglo-Indian community preferential employment in the upper and lower subordinate cadres. As a result, during the first half of the 20th century, the majority of guards, drivers, firemen, loco-foremen and line maintenance staff were Anglo-Indians who took enormous pride in their gleaming iron horses. They ran their trains with split-second punctuality, and even during the turmoil of the Quit India Movement, were resolute in their determination to keep the railways functioning in the teeth of demonstrations, processions and blockades. Without their unquestioning loyalty, the entire railway system would have been seriously crippled, if not completely paralyzed.

Social Activities

Before most of the Anglo-Indians left India in the years following Independence, the Railway Institute was the focal point of social activity. Every Railway Institute had an Entertainment

Committee which organized and ran whist drives, housie (bingo) nights, dances, amateur theatricals, costume parties, tin-and-bottle badminton tournaments and sports day events.

Apart from functions at the Railway Institute, Anglo-Indian railway communities celebrated Christmas in their own inimitable fashion. The lead up to the big day involved a special trip by one or more members of the Community to the nearest city – in my experience, Calcutta – where, armed with a shopping list for themselves and friends, they would troop off to the New Market to buy dress material and trimmings (for the house tailor to work with on a bungalow verandah), toys for the children, a selection of dried fruit and nuts, as well as barley sugar (striped candy), marzipan, and a Christmas pudding from one of the Calcutta confectioners like Nahums, Flurys or Trincas.

With Gran, Dad & Mum, Asansol, 1944

As a Community, the Anglo-Indians needed little or no excuse to whoop it up, and since everyone knew everyone else in the Railway colony, occasions such as birthdays, First Holy Communions, and weddings were celebrated with gusto.

Funerals were sombre affairs, but again almost the entire Railway Anglo-Indian community could be counted on to attend the service for one of its departed members.

Margaret Deefholts with her sister Phyllis in Calcutta, 1952

In the cooler winter months, there were organized picnics (sometimes by moonlight) and as shikar (hunting) was a popular sport, shooting parties would take off to the surrounding marshlands to bag duck, partridge and snipe. On big game shoots, overnight camps would be set up, and beaters (groups of local villagers) would "beat" the jungle with drums, sticks and noisy shouts, to funnel wild boar, deer, panther or tiger towards machaan platforms where hunters lay in wait.

The Railway Institute

The first time I attended the Railway Institute was in Allahabad over the Christmas season in '46. Housie (bingo) evenings, whist drives and various other social events were something of an eye-opener for me. As children we were 'seen and not heard' at home and were packed off to bed by 8 o'clock, but at the Institute, kids swarmed all over the place – and nobody seemed to mind if they stayed up until after midnight. Youngsters ran and slid along the French-chalked dance floor, babies sat on their grandmothers' laps and toddlers were fussed over by friends and families. A wind-up gramophone blared above the din and confusion, and the music was lively and rhythmic. So much more catchy than the classical nocturnes and études on our gramophone at home. Everyone, youngsters and oldsters, seemed to be having a wonderful time jitterbugging and Lambeth-walking around the floor!

The Deefholts' bungalow, Gymkhana Road, Jamalpur, 1948

Traveling by Rail

Probably the most delightful part of railway life for me as a child was the unmitigated thrill of traveling on the rails. And we did a great deal of this right through the '40s and '50s, as Dad sometimes took us "on line" (during our school holidays) when he went on tour to one of the outlying stations within his jurisdiction.

As a junior officer, he had an Officers' Carriage – a capacious four berth compartment with an attached kitchen and an alcove with two tiered sleeping berths for our cook and bearer.

My mother would pack a large wicker tiffin (food) hamper with provisions: bread, butter, eggs, jam, tea, sugar and condensed milk tins, and the cook would be dispatched to the local market each day for fresh meat, vegetables and fruit, while the O.C. stood parked on an off-platform siding. Remembering the sound of the wheels clacking over the points, the jog and sway of the carriage, the smell and prickle of coal dust on skin and scalp (this was in the days before diesel engines) and the taste of hardboiled eggs (smeared with sooty fingerprints!), still evokes a feeling of wistful nostalgia.

When my father became a Department Head, the Officers' Carriage was replaced by an Officers' Saloon – a 3-bedroom bogey with a wash basin in each bedroom, a private toilet and shower, a kitchen and pantry with a fridge, a dining area with a fold-away table, and a lounge with comfortably upholstered sofas and curtains framing the windows. Sometimes, though not always, the saloon was air conditioned rather than fan-cooled.

Indian railway first class carriages until the '60s were self-contained four berth compartments with their own attached toilets. These have all now disappeared and been replaced by relatively cramped four berth cubicles leading off a long corridor, with common toilets situated at each end. When on holiday, we traveled in those roomy first class compartments, and our meals – breakfast, lunch and dinner – were catered from either the railway restaurant car (now non-existent) or from railway catering establishments at junction stations. A meal order would be telegraphed down the line, and delivered at the next major train stop. Dining room contractors such as Kelners (north India) produced excellent meals, and their caramel custard was legendary!

When it was necessary to stay overnight before making a train connection, we were accommodated at the Railway Officers rest-rooms at the station. In those days they were impeccably clean, (although the rooms smelt of phenol swabbed floors!) and the Railway station dining rooms had heavy cutlery, and crockery/glassware embossed with the insignia of the Indian Railways. The bearers (waiters) wore starched white jackets, and their belts and turbans were surmounted by a badge or buckle with the Indian Railways logo.

For me, no return trip to India is complete without a train journey, even though the engines are diesel and the wheels no longer beat to the rhythm of our ayah's chant of "*Chay-chay paisa, chal-Calcutta!*" (six-six paise, go Calcutta!) and breakfast now comes pre-packaged in a soggy cardboard box containing an equally soggy "amlet" and leathery "toas". Gone forever too, is beef curry with fluffy scented rice – and also vanished, alas, is the best caramel custard in the universe!

Looking back to those early years of railway life, it seems to me that despite the upheavals that India was going through at the time, the days were unhurried and tranquil. Our household routine went on as usual; the servants were gentle, kindly and respectful. We were part of a gracious life style – much of it born out of an Anglo-Indian tradition that had endured for three centuries.

Today my parents have passed on, and my sister and I have been in Canada for over 35 years. Yet a part of us still remains in the hot, dusty plains of India and wraith-like dodges in and out of the shadows of that long vanished era of Railway life in the mid-1900s.

Excerpts from the book 'Haunting India'
Photographs courtesy: Margaret Deefholts

A Colony Called Home

Colleen Gantzer

We were 'Railway People'. And when we said that, we had said everything. It expressed who we were, what we did, how we behaved and dressed and spoke. We spoke a fast English patois. Many of the gentle folk of Wales had laid down the bedrock of our railways and their lilt influenced the rhythm of our speech.

Consequently, Railway People were distinct, and clannish. And they were governed by customs, traditions, conventions and taboos as rigid as those which held any clan together.

One of the unwritten laws was that Railway People did not really need to leave their circumscribed world. Everything you needed was there, particularly if it was a big railway colony centered around the great Junctions with their clanging, hooting Loco Workshops. These were the places where the huge, black engines, or locomotives, were repaired, refitted and restored to sound, steam-driven, health. The 'shops' were controlled by all-powerful Loco Foremen. They formed the steel backbone of the railways and though some of them came from Britain, the best-regarded ones were those who had cut their engineering teeth in the railways as 13-year-old apprentices: as Daddy had.

And because Daddy was a Loco Foreman when I was born, my memories of the railways were those of a privileged little girl sheltered by the aura and status of my father.

Fittingly, our house was huge. It had deep verandahs festooned with creepers covered in ice-cream pink flowers: they are still known as Railway Creepers. This blossom-draped house was set in enormous grounds at the edge of a vast field. On the far side of the field was the Institute, the center of the social lives of Railway People. Beyond it was the village and the rest of the world. Long before the Japanese realized the virtues of treating their employees as members of a closely-knit corporate family, the GIP, EIR and the BB&CI had nurtured this sense of belonging. Quite frankly, you belonged to your railway company, and your company belonged to you.

All this led to a very strange attitude among Railway People: "Why do that extra schooling, men? We can get good jobs without the SC: "The 'SC' was the Senior Cambridge School Leaving Certificate. If you had the build for it and were a good sportsman, officers weren't too strict about your age: "After all, he's a railway boy!" And so these teenaged boys tied a handkerchief around their heads, had their arms tattooed and began firing: shoveling coal into the engines.

In course of time they handled their own locomotives as shunters, moving wagons and coaches in the yards, were promoted to goods train drivers and hoped, in time, to rise through passenger train, express and, eventually, to the top of the heap as the elite Mail Train Drivers.

Railway people worked hard, but they also played hard. The Institute was the center of their relaxing hours. Here, every evening, the men and women gathered: the men to play billiards or tennis, the women to sit and gossip while the kids played around them. Children were never left at home, not even when the Institute ran its Christmas and New Year parties. They helped their parents decorate the "Inster" with flags, streamers, balloons and casuarina 'Christmas Trees' trimmed with cotton wool snow. They sat giggling on the sidelines while their elders danced. Railway society placed considerable stress on enjoying life without thinking of tomorrow. Why think of the future? Why save? The railways looked after you and when you had to retire you got your Provident Fund and, hopefully, your sons would have joined the Railways and your daughters would have married good railway men.

Thus, the social life of the Inster was a very important part of growing up in a Railway colony. And so we went to dances and treasure hunts, and took part in the annual sports organised by the Inster and we learnt, almost instinctively, exactly where to draw the line. These codes of conduct were not enforced by any law makers or Council of Elders. They had evolved and were accepted by everyone as the done thing. Everyone knew what everyone else did: it was a strong, mutually-supportive society. Railway people enjoyed themselves because their society ensured that liberty never deteriorated to license. Your neighbour would not be allowed to harm you.

Railway People lived for the day assured that the Railway would look after their tomorrows. So they boxed and played hockey and shot 'game' all up and down the line. They really lived life king-size because they had no aspirations outside their contentedly circumscribed lives.

The railway colony was a 'colony' in every way. It was a protected outpost of a unique civilization dedicated to just one aim: to keep those great puffing monsters moving efficiently, uninterruptedly, swiftly.

But generations of living in such a protected environment can be dangerous. When the railways were nationalized, the old commercial, competitive spirit melted away. The carefully cosseted lives of Railway People were exposed to meddling by those despised creatures, the 'babus' with pens stuck behind their ears and the books of Rules and Regulations as their Bibles. As a tough old mail driver with slate-grey eyes said to me, "What is the point of working, girl, if the khalasi can become a shunter because his father-in-law is the Minister's peon?" Reservations and socialist equality have no place in a revered hierarchical system in which only hard work and efficiency lets you climb the social ladder. Or so many Railway People believed.

So, as the winds of change blew through the Railways, long honoured traditions began to crumble, expectations began to change, people who had lived for generations in the carefully structured camaraderie of a railway colony suddenly found themselves faced with new, and distasteful, alien values where sycophancy, nepotism and the nudge-and-a-wink paid richer dividends than the outspoken honesty of the old days.

The Age of Innocence had gone and with it had vanished the sterling mores that had bound the old Railway colonies.

There are still very dedicated people who work in the railways but it has become very difficult to recognize Railway People.

This article was first published in The National Anglo-Indian Railway Convention Souvenir 2003, edited by Dr. Beatrix D'Souza

TRACKING DOWN MY CHILDHOOD RAILWAY MEMORIES

Rudy Otter

THE OLD 'LINE-CLEAR' operation, performed by drivers of steam-engined express trains sweeping non-stop through stations, was exciting to watch.

As a youth, I would lean out of our rattling first-class carriage window, squinting to avoid coal particles from entering my eyes, and see the driver (frequently my father) prepare to swoop into action.

Imagine the tension rising as the steam engine, with its protruding line-clear arm, is thundering towards a 'through' station. The steel arm scoops up the line-clear pouch from a trackside post. Pouch thwacks against the engine's side. Driver grabs the pouch. Whips it off the arm. Opens it. Checks the ball token's code, then throws the previously collected line-clear pouch into a stretch of netting at the other end of the station it has just hurtled through. It was like scoring a goal within a set number of seconds.

All express train drivers on the then single-track Dhond-to-Poona run, separated by six intermediate stations, were involved in the 'line- clear' routine and they had to be quick, otherwise they risked missing the station's net by several hundred yards. Every split-second counted, and the drivers accurately netted each throw – it was a skill that called for concentration, manual dexterity and speed of execution.

Oh, what memories! So many wonderful railway memories!

Isn't it amazing how we Anglo-Indians, many of whom like myself left India more than half a century ago, still feel so deeply attached to the land of our birth? We have India in our blood. We live and breathe India. We can reel off an inexhaustible array of memories spanning every facet of our early Anglo-Indian lives in vivid and enthusiastic detail.

Our attachment to India, after all these years, is a remarkable phenomenon. We find ourselves in a time-warp, unable or unwilling to sever the umbilical cord and blend without trace into our adopted environments of Britain, Australia, New Zealand, Canada, United States and elsewhere. Paradoxically our Community, spread all over the world, is now closer together than ever, thanks to superb magazines like *Anglos In The Wind* and excellent websites like *The Anglo-Indian Wallah* and many others.

The Anglo-Indian community in India was at its peak in the 1920s to 1940s. Our fathers and grandfathers worked on the many narrow and broad gauge railway systems that covered India in those days – I would say that at least 95 per cent of Anglo-Indians worked on the railways – as drivers, guards, firemen, ticket collectors, station masters, loco foremen, booking clerks, yard foremen, engine turners, fuel inspectors, permanent way inspectors and even in the exalted positions of Assistant Technical Superintendent (ATS) and Divisional Superintendent (DVS).

Our railway colony, Dhond, once teemed with Anglo-Indian families. I'll mention various surnames (reeling off surnames was a popular Anglo-Indian pastime, remember?) and some might well ring a bell with you. Here we go: Hill, McDonough, Routcliff, Menasse, Bolton, Adams, Gidney,

Gardner, Scott, O'Dowd, O'Leary, Gannon, Vaz, Furnell, Hayter, Warren, White, Thomas, Clabby, Reynolds, Cawdrey, DeMello, Sweeney, Crooks, Ford, Clough, Stevenson, Dean, Neal, Claygen, Carapeit, Durham, Ingles, Ellis, Speechley, Rodericks, Nyss, Judge, Monteiro, Alphonso, Rebeiro, Knight, Shepherd, Kennet, Baskett, Pires, Rose, Lewis, Montez, Witty, the muscular fireman Reggie Lincoln (one-time middle-weight weightlifting champion of India), Dunne, Hardaker, Carvalho, Saldanha, Lazarus, Joseph, Pavey, Galloway, Fox, of course Otter and many more.

Our parents and the Durhams started off as neighbours at the railway quarters in Dhond and became close buddies. Although both families had later been moved to other quarters in town, the deep friendship survived. Josephine Durham's mother, Mrs. Ingles, had the latest and most coveted hi-tech gadget in those days – a wind-up gramophone. She would rotate the handle and play such hit records as Daisy, Daisy... Don't Fence Me In... Red River Valley... I Wonder Who's Kissing Her Now?... It's A Long Way To Tipperary... Jealousy... My Happiness... Volare... Dreamboat...

Josephine's husband, Tommy, had several interests. He would go on various jungle shoots around Sholapur and invariably present us with legs of venison which our dear woman cook, nicknamed Fatty, would transform into succulent vindaloo and roast dishes. Tommy, a formidably talented snooker player, would win all the competitions in the European Railway Institute, then cross over the railway bridge to the Indian Railway Institute and thrash their snooker aces as well. (In those bygone days, Anglo-Indians could attend both European and Indian Institutes, but the Indians were restricted to the Indian Institute only, such were the "privileges" we Anglos enjoyed in Dhond).

Finally, Tommy was never known to miss a railway dance, and would re-arrange any obstructive train-driving shift to ensure he was free to jive and jitterbug on the European Institute's wooden dance floor, made smooth by AI youngsters who were encouraged to slide up and down to spread the sprinkled chalk.

'Monty' Montez was another great character at those Anglo-Indian dances. He was a jolly man who had been to England for a couple of years and returned with what we termed a 'stylish' accent. Full of jokes, he called out the numbers for the tombola sessions and also enlivened the dances by playing "In the Mood" on the institute piano. Oh, those happy institute days, so many warm and wonderful memories to savour – the whist drives, dances, sports functions, the New Year bonfires which we romped around, arms linked, singing Auld Lang Syne, followed by hugs and kisses.

Mary and Eric Adams were prominent in organising social events at Dhond's European Railway Institute. They would provide endless trays of corned beef sandwiches, meat patties, savouries and coffee, everything snapped up by a forest of eager hands.

Eric was the Institute's regular Father Christmas, and as a 7-year-old, proudly hugging my drum that the nice white-bearded old man wearing a bright red outfit had brought me all the way from Lapland, I innocently announced to all my starry-eyed pals that Santa was wearing "Mr. Adams's brown shoes". The adults within earshot erupted with laughter at my perceptive observation and shattered our treasured childhood illusion forever while the heavily disguised Mr. Adams shook with mirth!

Mary Adams, a tall and friendly lady, was a perfect hostess, moving around the dance hall, chatting with everyone, laughing and joking. She loved to stand in the middle of the dance hall and sing her favourite song – "Keep young and beautiful if you want to be loved" – which always drew a hearty ovation.

Then there were those picnics and hair-raising swimming sessions in the great River Bhima which was reputed to be visited often by stray crocodiles.

Jokers would point at the water and shout, "I saw something black moving down there!" and the swimmers would break Olympic records as they splashed away in the opposite direction.

I still remember hiring bicycles with my pals at 2 annas an hour from a market shop and having races along Dhond's then deserted roads. I remember climbing roofs and shinning up trees for a game called 'Jack the Monkey'. Occasionally we would disturb crows' nests and for days afterwards have to run for cover as the birds waited to fly down and whack us with their wings. We also sprinted about with steel hoops, played gilli-danda, sword-fenced with sticks. And what about attempting the circus balancing act of 'walking' on those large earth-flattening rolling stones? All we boys also fancied the idea of becoming the next Joe Louis. One of the rooms in our railway quarters was reserved for boxing bouts. With gloves bought from a Poona sports shop, I had ferocious slugging matches with George Joseph, Clive Judge, Peter Adams, Walter Scott and Tony Saldanha...

My late father, who liked to be known by his initials "R.T." Otter, was born and brought up in Cuddapah, Andhra Pradesh, and spent virtually the whole of his GIP Railway career in Dhond, retiring in 1951 as an express train driver of those sleekly maintained steam engines. He loved the railway and took a particular interest in the GIP Regulations Book which he studied for hours while sitting in the verandah on his favourite easychair with those extended leg-supports. He would paste in the amendments he received with great care and kept the book up-to-date, becoming such an expert that other railway workers would seek his help and advice whenever they had a work problem.

Memories, so many memories! I recall we Anglo-Indian families in Dhond walking up and down the station platforms, surrounded by tea vendors shouting "*Chai! Garam chai!*", newspaper sellers, pan wallahs and fruit sellers. We enjoyed spending our evenings looking into newly arrived passenger trains to see it we recognised any Anglos passing through on their way to Sholapur, Bangalore, Ahmednagar.

In our day, in India, compartments were arranged in three classes – Upper Class, Inter and Lower Class, and most Anglo railway families were given Upper Class travel passes.

Hey, what about those Brandon's restaurants on railway stations? They were superb eateries specialising in masala fried fish dishes as well as biriyanis dotted with yellow/red/green grains of rice. 1 can still smell the delicious aroma of Brandon's food filling the air as you walked in.

I cannot end without saluting one vital section of railway employees.

Life back in the old railway days in India was comparatively safe for the Anglo-Indian goods-train driver. He was accompanied by the fireman as well as the oilman (or *argwallah*). The three men felt secure in one another's company while they went about their duties on their hissing steam engine.

But what about the guard, on his own, tacked on to the end of a goods train consisting of 50 to 60 wagons more than half a mile away down the line?

It must have been particularly nerve-wracking when a goods train halted at an outer signal in the middle of the night, leaving the guard in his open van surrounded by frightening wildlife screeches and inexplicable movements through the foliage. On top of this, the lone and vulnerable guard probably had to contend with the sudden appearance of dacoits brandishing knives and demanding money.

Correct me if I'm wrong but I seem to remember that the two doors on either side of the guard's van had no bolts, so a guard could not protect himself from invaders, and there was no emergency alarm, as far as 1 know, that linked him to the driver. The only time the driver, fireman or oilman would suspect something amiss was if the guard failed to shine his lamp.

How, I wonder, did the old goods-train guards cope with life on their own, at the far end of those very long trains? Did they encounter any dangerous situations? Were they attacked by dacoits or wild animals while the goods train waited at an outer signal, in the middle of nowhere, perhaps stuck in a jungle? Their recollections, or the experiences of their fellow goods' guards, are sure to make fascinating reading.

Our Days In The Sun

Manobina Dasgupta

Memories of growing up in railway colonies in the various small towns, in the 1940s to the early '70s are enduring. Our lives were sheltered, peaceful and impervious to the chaos, cacophony, and often political tumult outside in various parts of India.

The colonial style bungalows set in acres of land with trees, lawns edged with flower-beds, lily pools, and a vegetable garden at the back were safe from the intrusion of the outside world. These colonies were built around the focal point of the "railway station" and the workshop referred to as the "works". Everything was meticulously planned and laid down to detail, including all facilities for the railway staff that lived there.

There were churches, and the local school that was run by Anglo-Indian ladies. It would be wrong if I did not mention that these ladies were the backbone of most English-medium schools all over India. They were highly regarded for their English language skills, as well their commitment to discipline. As music and sports teachers they were very dedicated, and often, extremely proficient.

The railway hospital or dispensaries offered prompt service for all railwaymen and their families. Here too the Anglo-

Indian nursing staff was very valuable. The "Matron" was a figure of awe and reverence.

It would be remiss of me, if I were not to mention the Railway Institute and Club, where weekends were spent in games and other social activities. They were colonial to the core. The billiards room would often have wood panelled walls, where the sound of the cue hitting the red ball would accentuate the silence. Friday evenings would be movie nights and were well attended.

I particularly loved the game of 'Housie' or Bingo. Mother had enormous winning luck in Housie, or at the card table, or in lucky dip stalls at the fetes. Once at a fete, at the 'Ring the Duck' stall, she aimed well, and like a lasso put a ring around a frightened duck's neck. It was not easy, as it was difficult to single out any one duck from among twenty scared ducks running all together in a frenzied manner inside the little wood and bamboo stockade built for them. We were very excited at her winning, but our faces fell, when the man in charge of the game picked up the petrified duck with dilated eyes and held it out to us to take home. Our reluctance set off much mirth, as onlookers kept telling us not to 'chicken out', as someone else might grab the duck and carry it away to have duck curry or vindaloo the next day. Our bungalow peon came to our rescue, and brought it home.

We never ate the duck, and it joined Mother's menagerie with its dogs, hens, guinea pigs, rabbits, cows, as well as a macaca monkey. The monkey was a discovery. One day, when our maid Hema went to dust and clean the guest bedroom, she was startled to see this monkey sitting on the dressing table, looking at her own reflection in the mirror and watching her image imitate her. It was not frightened of Hema, and it seemed, that it was used to human contact. Hema was excited and wanted to keep the monkey as a pet calling her Rukmini. Mother made enquiries, and it was discovered that the "*bundarwala*" or monkey-man to whom Rukmini had belonged could not afford to feed his monkeys, and released them. He just went away leaving them eating biscuits at a tea-stall near the railway station. Mother arranged for Rukmini's vaccination shots. Rukmini also bit Hema's hand in the struggle while she was being held down for her shots. Hema kept her anyway, but took a tetanus injection too.

All this was possible in smaller mofussil towns, with the many trolley-men, gardeners, bungalow peon, *dhobi* and other staff. We had to part with our menagerie, and only keep our dogs after Father was transferred to another city.

The children in the colony played together and we also played with the children from the "outhouses". They taught me to climb the mango and litchi trees in our bungalow compound and to use the catapult with precise accuracy.

While inside the colonies, life went on peacefully, and outside, the political upheaval of the times was to impact our lives soon. India became free, and the demography of the country changed – she lost her innocence and simplicity. It was not long after that the steam era came to an end ... the steam engines headed to scrap iron yards.

Of my Anglo-Indian friends, Avril and her family left to a grim post-war Britain. In her Father's conversations, he had always spoken of the 'home country'. His family was fiercely loyal to the Imperial rule and a "mother country" they had never experienced. In India they were sandwiched between the "ruling class" of the "*pukka sahib*" and those whom they ruled over – "the natives". After a year in England, she wrote with a touch of disillusionment that life was not easy – the grass may look greener on the other side of the fence, but it's just as hard to cut. She would cherish in her memory her friends and her "days in the sun". The poignancy cannot be belied – I never heard from her again. But, I am so glad, that a few stayed behind like the Gwynnes – Jennifer and Carol in Madras, and the Pereiras – Elaine and Leslie Pereira of Calcutta . They enrich the fabric of my life.

I had never thought that the timeless Railway Spirit would end this way – but it is the way of the world, the transient quality of our lives. From a railway carriage it would seem like – "each a glimpse, and gone forever."

The Arakonam Railway Institute

Alistair Reneaux

I stand here lost, deserted and decrepit,
No longer am I good enough and fit,
No more the host of joyful celebration,
Such is my fate, such my situation.

Weddings I've hosted, many dances too,
Under my watch the lads and lasses grew;
At Christmas time, I was so full of cheer,
It surely was the best time of the year!

Alone with heavy heart I now recall
Crowning the May Queen hosting the June Rose ball,
Admiring colourful kids, in fancy dress,
Smiling when priest, the wedding cake would bless.

I was the heart and soul of the festive season,
For all the railway folk, I was the reason
They could shout "Housie", dance the night away,
Will fun and frolic, wheel of fortune play.

If my red brick walls, my creaky wooden floor
Could only speak of folks from long ago,
Who filled me with their music, song and dance,
Their tears and laughter – that was true romance!

Oh tell me why I'm left to stand and cry,
Watch unkempt grass surround me, wither and die,
I wonder where those lovely folk have gone
I gaze at the tracks, forsaken and forlorn.

I see new trains take people here and there,
A silent sentinel, I stand and stare,
Look back in time when I could proudly boast,
Of every railway town, I was the toast!

A 1970 photo of the Anglo-Indian Association, Arakonam Branch.

Sitting: L to R: Audrey D'Cruz, young Jean D'Cruz, Agnes White, Doris Nicholas, Rita Tennant, Phyllis Doyle, Dulcie Emanuel and Mrs. Moore. Standing L to R: E.R. D'Cruz, D. Emanuel, William Doyle and Mr. O'Brien.

Photo Courtesy: Eugene D'Cruz (Sydney)

Uncle Tom's Cabin

Bryan O. Peppin

My uncle Tom was the kind of man you seldom see: medium height, gaunt to an extreme limit that makes you feel even a little less flesh would make the bone-weight of the body unsupportable, but of such genial spirits that you never really noticed his sparse frame. He had deep-set, dark eyes that never lost their dream-like expression. To me he was one of those patriarchs steeped in wisdom and anchored in well-satisfied self-respect.

Like most of my relatives, and perhaps as in most other Anglo-Indian families Tom Brewart was a railway-man. Looking at him set me imagining that a blend of steel and coal burned at the core of every true Anglo-Indian. Uncle Tom once mentioned this himself, and when I pressed him for more information on the subject, he said, "Boy, the Railway is the life-line of our Community. We were the pioneers; we set the wheels in motion; we brought the different Indias together; we nurtured this monolithic organisation and gave it meaning; but, when the hardest part of the job was done, we were, more or less, jettisoned. Still, the railway is part of our heritage. Remember, always remember, without tradition no one can survive.

"The steam-engine years," Uncle Tom continued, "marked the heyday of our people. Boys only waited to complete their elementary school to be inducted as khalasis. Sometimes it took years to be upgraded as second fireman, but, inevitably, almost everyone made it. Then to first fireman and finally to the coveted post of driver. I too had my internship, over a period of ten years, but by keenly watching my cabin-mates, I learnt all the ropes, even as the shovelling and collecting of the 'all-clear' keys toughened my body. I wanted very much to be my own man, and at the age of thirty-two, that dream became a reality.

"Right from the beginning, Madras was the hub around which the entire railway machine in South India revolved. It was with immense pride that the loco drivers of my day rode in state into the artistic marvels of Central and Egmore stations. The drivers of mail and express trains, hauled by Mallard Express steam engines or even the Ellerman Lines specials, all of them wore spanking white uniforms just to show how really clean the foot plates were. When the crews checked in for duty they would report hours before time, just to see that the engines were spick and span, the brass fittings gleaming burgundy and gold against the thunderous blackness of the boiler and the quick-silver sheen of the perch. And it was an unwritten rule that if the driver reported sick, his firemen would follow suit. So there they were, at Cochin and Shoranur, Podanur and Erode, Madurai and Trichinopolly, Villupuram and Arkonam, Kazipet and Waltair, these bands of men, intent on their jobs, intense in their love for their rolling-stock, intrepid in the carrying out of their duties. You had the Bentleys, Gouldings, Vieyras, D'Cruzs, Paynes, D'Sylvas, Platels, Smiths, Cleurs, Rozarios, and oh-so-many more.

"Every driver," Uncle Tom went on, downing a generous peg of rum-and-water. "Every driver had his own signal, while leaving station or returning, to tell the family in the railway quarters that he was on board. The whistle would delicately and accurately identify the respective driver so that, especially on the down run, 'chotta' and coffee could be kept ready. After the porter had secured the driver's box in the running room, and after the goodbyes to his mates, the man would be home in fifteen minutes or so, either walking or bicycling the distance to the lines. Long before the next run, the driver would be back at the yards, supervising and tending the machine that was his life, face aglow because of the glittering steel of the coupling rod, crank, connecting rod and combination lever, and at the burnished gold of the levers and gauges within the cabin. The exercise came to an end with an inspection of the blood-red buffers, front and back, and a check of the water-filler, with the hand-rail for support."

Another pull from his tumbler and Uncle Tom's eyes took on a glaze that to me indicated nothing but reminiscence. Since I, too, a long time ago, had adopted his thorough-going philosophy of simple living and high drinking, I knew the mood very well. Many drinkers are mistaken for drunks, but that's because only the chosen few really know the difference. Uncle also had words of caution: "Beggars," he said, "cannot be boozers." And in the course of my studies, I came across the heady advice: "Drink, don't think," which still seems a very fine alternative. Uncle Tom was quite certain that though many drivers may have had fire-water in their bellies when on duty, they were rarely involved in accidents, since theirs was a labour of love, of devotion, and of honour. "That really isn't the case today, is it?" he asked, dreamily.

"When I was in my cabin, riding the foot-plate, I was on top of the world, yet grounded in reality because of the direction-finding tracks. I knew every siding, every signal tower, every culvert, every span of every bridge. Every running-room had its own speciality and the cooks in those days were tops: idlis and kurma, dosas and fish curry, parottas and vindaloo, idiappam and paya, appam and errichi curry, all sent down with metre-long draughts of chai or kaapi."

The dreamy look had now given way to a sleepy-tired one. "Son," Uncle Tom said, "it's a good thing, at times, to keep the past before you, because there's so much that can be learnt from it – both good and bad. But it's a terrible thing to let the past dominate the present; that makes one brood, makes one sinister, makes one an escapist. So let me end this chat of ours with an anecdote:

"In those days there used to be foot-plate inspections. British officers would poke around, looking for minute faults. One morning I had just steamed into Central from Erode and had given Kannan, a khalasi, charge of my box. My firemen had also joined me for tea at the dining room further down the station. From out of nowhere a British officer pounced on Kannan, demanding the names of the crew. 'Who is the driver?' thundered the Britisher. 'Brute, Saar,' whined the khalasi, noticing the flummoxed expression on the officer's face. 'And the firemen?' 'Step in son and peep in, Saar,' said Kannan, a little more confidently. 'What? Speak up!' said the officer. Kannan repeated: 'Step in son and peep in.' 'Insolent fool! I'll see the end to this!' snorted the white man, as he swivelled and marched away. Half-way back to the engine, I noticed the officer's heightened colour. Believing that introductions were in order, I said, 'Sir, I'm Brewart, the driver. And these are my firemen, Stephenson and Peppin.'"

This article was first published in The National Anglo-Indian Railway Convention Souvenir 2003, edited by Dr. Beatrix D'Souza

The Ballad of the Engine Driver

Isaac Mathison

There goes the engine driver
And fantasy runs wild!
To the man-in-the-street on a rail-coach seat,
He's one of a special tribe.
He's a hard-living, hard-loving, big boozing man,
A regular ne'er-do-well.
Who drives his train like a super-jet plane,
And crashes it straight into hell!

But to family, colleagues and loved ones,
He's just the man next door.
He loves his wife, adores his kids,
A gentleman to the core.
He's a hardworking, home-loving, God-fearing man,
Who wouldn't hurt a fly.
He's much maligned, misunderstood,
As the following verses imply...

Swiftly, silently, safely,
As the miles go rushing by,
Uphill, down dale, past mountain and vale,
Through forest or desert dry,
As you blissfully dream your dreamless dreams,
Or watch the world slip by,

The man at the helm is alert and calm,
As you list to his lullaby.

In the bustle of day or stillness of night,
You're safe in his calloused hands.
In the blistering heat or cold, cold sleet,
Near home-town or far-away land.
For him there's no summer, winter or spring,
No blizzard or blinding rain,
The only goal for him, dear soul,
Is your comfort, your safety, your train!

He may not resemble a dashing filmstar,
He probably looks like your dad!
His skin is rough, his hands are tough,
But his brain's as sharp as a blade.
He has years and years of experience,
And has weathered many a storm.
He's been through the mills of life's valleys and hills,
And is worthy to pilot you home.

Before he leaves home for the journey,
The family gathers around,
To ask the Almighty to bring him back safely
To family hearth and home.
For, like you, he has kiddies and loved-ones,
Waiting for dad to return,
Waiting, watching, praying, longing,
For their dear face to come home.

You usually take it for granted
When your train arrives safe and on time,
But for him it's a moment of joy and contentment
To see happy faces go by.
To him you're not just a traveller,
But a son, a mother, a friend,

Who has placed in his hands, your future plans:
That trust he guards to the end!

Swiftly, silently, safely,
As the miles go rushing by,
Uphill, down dale, past mountain and vale,
Through forest or desert dry,
Remember friend! Remember!
If perchance a mishap takes place,
It's the man at the head who'll be the first dead,
For him it's the final race!

So friend, do not treat him coldly,
Or of him talk in lighter vein,
His job's not to carry just you and your family,
But hundreds like you on his train!
Every mile, every foot of the journey,
Every twist, every turn of the line,
With care and precision, split-second decision,
Devotion to duty, concern for your safety,
Sure of his skill, but trusting th' Almighty,
He'll be back,
Safely home
And-on-time!!!

His Last Trip:
Isaac Mathison
on his retirement day

Photo courtesy: Isaac Mathison

A Railwayman Looks Back

Noel Thomas

In April 1957, not yet seventeen, I stood before the Selection Board. The written test was over and the interview was coming to an end.

"Could you name some of India's first hockey Golden Olympians?" asked the Chairman.

Only Anglo-Indian names came to my mind: "Penniger, Hammond, Allen, Norris – "

"Anyone else?" he cut me short.

"Dhyan Chand, Sir," I said, redeeming myself. AME Mr. Delahoid, also on the panel, smiled at me as I left the room.

Soon after, I was taken on as an Apprentice in Khurda Road Loco Shed. Jossy Lovery was the Head Fitter. He maintained a dignified presence and we trainees looked up to him. Of course, there were friendly supervisors like George Blanche, Joe Trindade and others.

There were many steam engines at the Loco Shed. Some of them had famous names like Engine No. 258, GCS which was called Francis Drake and others were called Bellerophon and Dreadnought; the only "Indian" named engine was "Juggernaut", quite aptly, I thought, Khurda being so close to Puri, the shrine of Jagganath.

The very first time I climbed on to one of these black beauties, I got badly scalded through shoes and socks. As I was climbing up, the steam-man opened the injector and the steamy overflow came directly onto my foot. The scar on my left instep is still an indelible impression, a reminder of my steam days.

After a hard day's work, we always had our fun in the evenings. But after this mishap, I still remember Dr. Eustace Braganza frowning his displeasure at me as I hobbled along from table to table at the Parochial Hall Whist Drive. Yet, very professionally, he kept me on the sick list for a month, till my foot was completely healed.

Noel with daughter Rowena on his Retirement Day

On functionless evenings, fireman Joe Doll and I would take on Jossy Lovery and AFO Wadia, in a couple of bridge rubbers. The stakes were "Sev, Ghatia and Chai". I never played cards for money because my father, Alec, hated cards, calling them 'misfortunate', though on the rare occasion we persuaded him to substitute for a deal or two, his hand was flushed with aces, kings and trumps.

Noel's 2-year-old grandson Jordan Pereira in the cab of a diesel locomotive

Well, Joe and I had a lot of "hot stuff" at Jossy's and Wadia's expense. At the end of the game, Jossy, the more accomplished player of the two, would dissect and analyse and hold Wadia responsible for the loss. Jossy was a typical Anglo-Indian, boss in the shed, but a friend and equal in the "Inster".

Sardar Mangal Singh, a Sikh, was KUR's Loco Foreman, in fact, the first non-AI to hold the post, but in keeping with the tradition, he maintained the dignity and decorum of his office. When he came out on his rounds, the shed froze into silence and except for the hiss of steam and the thump of Gene Leake's sledge hammer in the smithy, no human sound could be heard. The Loco Foreman could afford to walk tall. He was the monarch of all he surveyed; he was, all in all, a powerful person.

The Loverys on a picnic (1970s)
Back row L to R: Peter, Kay with baby Deborah D'Brass,
Joan & Jossy Lovery, Penny D'Brass and Jonathan Lovery (with guitar)
Front row: L to R: Carlyle, Raymond, Christopher Lovery
and Annamarie D'Brass

Photo Courtesy: Peter Lovery (Toronto)

At the shed, one picked up stories that became legends over the years. An all-time favourite anecdote was how Robert Callaghan got a job at the shed. In the 1930s, Robbie, a young lad at that time, went to KUR Loco Shed to collect a bandy (discarded piston ring) which the mistry had promised him. He was about to collect his trophy when the Loco Foreman emerged from his chamber on his morning rounds. He was a typical rough, tough and gruff Anglo-Indian Loco Foreman. The mistry took off, but the young lad stood rooted to the spot.

"Come here, Sonny!" bellowed the gaffer.

"Good morning, Uncle," said the lad. "I came for a bandy."

The stern, rugged countenance broke into a half smile. The Foreman saw before him a bright, healthy, spunky young specimen, who, in his vision, could well be part of the BNR's future.

"Bandy!" he roared. "You want something better than that – come back tomorrow and I'll give you a job!"

Obtaining his father's instant approval, Robbie went the next day and was appointed as a Shed Cleaner. He retired as a Mail Driver.

I was just getting the hang of Boiler washout, ROH, MOH, Poppet valves, Joko valves, Caprotti valves, Stephenson's Link Motion, Walshaert's Valve Gear and wheeling arrangements of 2-8-2, 4-6-0, 4-8-2, when I found myself in another railway zone at Jamalpur, a premier Loco Workshop and training center on the Eastern Railway. On the 14th of October 1958, I entered Queen's Road Hostel, Jamalpur, to a hot reception, a veritable baptism of fire. Ragging was in full swing, both physical and mental, but it was systematic and well-organised, without the sadistic excesses one hears of these days.

"Do you play hockey?" asked a senior.

"Yes, and a bit of cricket too," I answered.

"You're an AI?" asked another senior, in disbelief. I realised then that I had something to prove to them. Ragging is now considered brutal and inhuman and is banned, but the ragging I experienced seemed to be an effective method to remove complexes and it has played a major role in establishing the well-known Jamalpur bond of brotherhood.

As apprentices we had 9 months of workshop training and 3 months of technical school. Jamalpur was a "Royal" railway town... Queen's Road, King's Road, Prince's Road, Albert Road, Victoria Road, well-maintained bungalows, a sports stadium, two Institutes, one with a swimming pool and band stand, 3 churches, a golf course, bowling green and a well-equipped hospital.

Apprentice Engineers Club, Jamalpur
Jamalpur Hockey League Champions 1960-1962
Standing L to R: Elston Fernandez, Noel Thomas, A. Majumdar, Pat Caszo, Arjun Wali, Mervyn Robinson, V S.Singh, Michael Kumar and Glyn Netto.
Sitting L to R: Randolph Baker (Capt), R. S. Mathur (V.Pres)
U Mahadevan (Pres) Trevor Perrier (Sports Secy)
Ground: P.B. Das, Parimal Sarkar and Bokul Bhatta.

Hostel life was enjoyable. On a monthly stipend of Rs. 110, we paid Rs. 35 as mess charge, but were served by liveried bearers and the food was substantial. Our "Saturday Special" dinners featured pilaus and dessert. There were less than ten of us AIs but we held our own and, though outnumbered by other communities, were respected for our prowess in sport, music and for our free intermingling. We were acceptable to all. The hostel had a makeshift AI band, with Aelred Murphy on the clarinet, Trevor Perrier on the harmonica and Pat "Boone" Caszo crooning. These musicians later joined the famous "Minstrels" band of Calcutta. We even staged an English Play in the Central Institute and, aided by a few talented colleagues, I was editing an in-house magazine. Many of us were elected captains of various disciplines. Harry Lopez was elected General Secretary of the Club, the first AI in many years to achieve this distinction. Mervyn Robinson was an outstanding student, and years later Darryl Burke's name was engraved in the Roll of Honour as the outstanding student of his batch. He was a Calcutta boy. Trevor Perrier, from Jhansi, was elected Sports Secretary. He was a brilliant center forward in hockey and also represented the Eastern Railway in cricket.

I did make it to the hockey team and what a team it was! The photograph (*left*) shows seven AIs in the team, but missing are some outstanding players like Terence Joseph, Errol Dundon, Clarrie Clarke and Roy Dias. Terence lost an eye playing in the Kaivan Cup at Calcutta. He is now a qualified and experienced metallurgist in Seattle, USA. Jamalpur used to enter in the Beighton Cup too.

Jamalpur had a few special-class Anglo-Indian apprentices. There were three during my time – Ron Rebeiro, Blair Williams and Norbert D'Souza. Some other famous Jamalpur sportsmen were boxers Laurie Carr and Bob Cranston, hockey players Dickie Carr, Ginger Clarke and Sargie Paul.

There were many Anglo-Indians in the Jamalpur Workshop. I can't name all of them here. But some of the AI officers and foremen I can remember are: Rae, Ducasse, Ollenbach, Sealy, Namey, Simpson, Robbins, Mackertich, D'Souza, Daly, Stockman, and Gomes.

One morning, as I entered the main workshop gate, I heard the Machine Shop Foreman, Samuels, asking his counterpart, Mr. G.G. Bull, "Is it a bull or a cow?" The question stopped all the incoming supervisors in their tracks. (Mrs. Bull had delivered a baby that morning!). The answer, when it came, was drowned in the many shouts of congratulations directed at the slightly embarrassed, yet very proud father.

* * *

In October 1962, batchmate Elston Fernandes and I were given a rousing send off at Jamalpur railway station by a noisy apprentice crowd. The main feature of these farewell ceremonies was the traditional toss up in the air three times to the accompaniment of loud cheers and "Hurrahs", a spectacle enjoyed by everyone who happened to be on the platform at that time.

This was an annual event, senior apprentices leaving Jamalpur at the end of the honeymoon period, to enter a new, responsible phase of life. Elston and I were posted as chargemen in the Diesel Loco Shed at Gaya.

With hearts too full for words, we sat silently in the Jamalpur-Gaya passenger train for sometime, then prepared to bunk it out for the night. Just before we stretched out, a policeman travelling along with us, warned all the passengers to be careful of their belongings. "This line is notorious for thefts," he said. "They don't even spare your chappals."

We awoke next morning to the sound of the policeman shouting and swearing in the choicest Hindi invective. His footwear (boots and stockings) were missing – only his!

Gaya, where Gautham Buddha found enlightenment, was in Dinapore Division in the Grand Chord section of the Eastern Railway. Elston and I were given a room in the Diesel Training School (once the European Institute), on Hindley

Road. The shed at Gaya was the first broad gauge main line diesel shed in the Indian Railways, set up in 1957.

The Diesel Training School offered conversion courses, from steam to diesel, for drivers and technicians of all railway zones. Many Anglo-Indians from the South were trained there... Arthur Morgan of Bitragunta, Reggie "Killer" Francis from Vijayawada, Haido Morris from Mysore, Austin Nicholas from Gooty and others trained along with me. The chief instructor was Bertie Pelegrim, who was an expert in diesel locomotion. Originally from Bangalore, he had a lovely voice. We used to encore his rendition of some old-time favourites like "Till" and "Begin the Beguine".

Across the road from the training school were the traffic quarters, where some guards by the name of Remedios, Starling, Jacobs, Peterson and a ticket examiner, "Jumbo" Rozario stayed.

Gaya had an extreme climate. The summer was intolerable with the hot wind blowing across the plains. The locals used to stare at me as I walked in the midday sun to and from duty, normally dressed. I thought it was they who looked funny, covered from head to toe in the scorching heat. Only when I heard comments like "*Beta, Mar Jayega*" (You'll die, Sonny) that I began to worry.

I was walking back to my "digs" one hot afternoon, passing the quarters of the American Service Engineers (we had purchased locomotives from America) when one of them, Clements, called out to me, "Hey, Noel, come and have a drink!" He must be crazy or joking, I thought; but stepping in, I found Clements and his buddies with a big jar of juice on the center table, from which they were filling up their glasses, sipping and enjoying the drink. He offered me a glass; I found it delicious, but soon realised that my American friends were having a refined version of our own Anglo-Indian mango fool, an effective antidote and preventive for sunstroke.

I started taking it myself and it helped me survive the hot summer months.

By this time, my younger brother Eustace had joined the Eastern Railways as an APWI in the same Grand Chord section. He used to trolley and camp frequently overnight in the ghat section of the Grand Chord, a stretch of 22 kms from Gujhandi to Gurpa, with an awe-inspiring, steep gradient, 3 long tunnels, 4 major bridges, 17 steep curves, high rocky cuttings and dense forest. Eustace recalls trying to sleep in a tent at night while the gangmen kept a fire burning continuously to discourage visits from the denizens of the jungle. At times, they heard the roar of the big cat, the grunt of the wild boar and the thud of the tipsy black bear, falling from the mahua tree after feasting on the intoxicating fruit. Watching the bear's antics, the Santhals got wise, resulting in the birth of a new indigenous brew called "mahua".

Eustace remembers an incident while travelling in the ghat section. In his words, "In August 1971, as APWI Gomoh, I was foot-plating by engine cab of the Pathankot Express between Gomoh and Gaya. The driver was Frankie Joseph of Gomoh, a genial soul who kept chatting with me while driving. As the train passed Gujhandi and entered the Ghat Section, Frankie's chatter ceased abruptly. It was a different Frankie Joseph I saw now. He stood motionless, eyes fixed ahead and just before we entered the first tunnel, he began to sing, 'Nearer my God to Thee'. He kept singing this hymn till we came out of the third tunnel and cleared the ghat section. Then Frankie started talking again, but mostly about various hazards like landslides, falling trees, overhead cables and rail fractures. While trolleying on the section, I came across the words, 'Jesus Saves' engraved on one of the milestones."

Frankie Joseph is no more. His son, Freddie, works in the commercial department of the divisional office at Dhanbad. Eustace retired as Divisional Engineer, Dhanbad, and has settled there.

Interestingly, the very first Rajdhani Express of the Indian Railways between Calcutta and Delhi, travelled over the Grand Chord route. Craker and Toker, both Anglo-Indians, were the first to drive the train on its inaugural run in 1969.

After electrification of the Grand Chord, the diesel shed at Gaya shifted to Patratu in March '64. Patratu was located in the Central India Coalfield (CIC) section of the Eastern Railway, in Hazaribagh district of Bihar, close to Ranchi. Four stations up the line was McCluskieganj, then known as the El Dorado of the Anglo-Indians.

McCluskieganj was an hour away by train. I had been there several times with loco inspectors Willie Young, Noel Ramsbotham, and Ronnie Miller. We met old residents like the Thipthorpes. Mrs. Thipthorpe was famous for her preserves, jams and pickles. There were beautiful houses on both sides of the tracks. One was called the "Doll's House"; it is said that a father built this house for his little daughter, making it an exact replica of her favourite toy. Some say the daughter herself recreated the toy she loved. It was the prettiest building in the Ganj.

One day, I went alone, stayed at the guest-house and had a long chat with Bill Kearney, who with his wife, was running the guest house. They were among the first settlers. Bill was well-built, with striking blue eyes, now bereft of sight, but which seemed to light up when he narrated tales of the Ganj. I wish I had taken down even half of what he had said. He was a retired railway officer from pre-Independence days.

In the early '50s, the General Manager of the Eastern Railway was inspecting the CIC section. The GM's special was scheduled to run through McCluskieganj (it was only a flag station of no commercial importance at that point in time), enroute to Khelari, further down the line, to hold a meeting with officials of the Associated Cement Company over there.

As the train approached McCluskieganj, the driver of the Special was surprised to hear the GM's voice on the intercom asking him to stop at McCluskieganj. So, he stopped. The GM, K.G.Mukherjee, better known as "King George" Mukherjee because of his regal bearing and Anglicised manners, jumped down on to the low platform and made for the station building, with his shocked entourage following him. Suddenly, he changed direction and went straight to the railway tea stall. Mrs. Bertha Kearney was pouring tea into khullars (earthen cups), lined in a row when someone whispered, "GM Sahib." She looked up to see an immaculately dressed man, who wished her the time of the day and asked, "How is Bill keeping?"

"Quite well, Sir," replied Mrs. Kearney.

"Where is he now?" asked the GM.

"In the guest house, Sir," replied the lady.

The GM paused in contemplation. Then, his secretary discreetly reminded him that they were running behind schedule and it wouldn't be nice to keep the ACC officials, important railway users, waiting.

"Give my regards to Bill," the GM said, turned around and walked majestically back to his salon. Signals were exchanged, a whistle blew and the GM's Special chugged out of McCluskieganj. It is said the GM was in good spirits that day. Bill Kearney was his mentor when "KG" joined as a young probationer officer. Mrs. Kearney ran the tea stall for many years, even after Bill had passed on. She offered the passengers not only a cup of good tea, but home-baked bread and biscuits too.

Patratu was a beautiful, but backward place. The diesel railway quarters was a virgin colony, infested with scorpions and snakes. I was called by the doctor to his quarters one night. There I saw one of my colleagues, Venu, who was bitten by a krait. The doctor had only tied a torniquet. I asked him whether he had the anti-venom serum. He took me aside and confessed his inexperience. He had the serum but was not sure how to administer it. I called for the jeep and brought the more experienced Dr. Bose from the steam loco colony. He gave Venu two injections, anti-venom and anti-tetanus. We propped him up on an easy chair. Dr. Bose advised us to keep him awake.

Meanwhile, the news had spread. A noisy bhajan party arrived from the Basti close to the shed. The leader claimed to know powerful mantras, which would nullify the effect of the poison. They wanted Venu to sit on the ground in their midst, while they performed the rituals. I didn't agree to this proposal and a fierce argument ensued. The leader accused me of obstructing a certain cure and warned me that I would be responsible if Venu didn't survive. I was unfazed and the stalemate continued. Suddenly, it dawned on me that Venu being an orthodox Brahmin, the mantras and rituals could have a soothing, psychological effect and keep him awake, as the doctor ordered. I told the leader of the group, "We will shift his chair in the position you want. Go ahead with your mantras, but don't touch him and don't give him anything to eat or drink." He was looking to save face and so readily agreed. The chanting carried on throughout the night into the wee hours. Venu twice complained of severe headache and nausea, but by daybreak he said he was feeling better. Dr. Bose examined him and declared him out of danger. Needless to add, the bhajan party took full credit for the cure!

Patratu was lacking in civic and other amenities – no school, public transport, markets or recreational facilities. Though fairly well-placed, I couldn't keep my mother with me – she needed good medical attention, which was non-existent.

In 1971, I met and married Sheila Bertram at Khurda Road. By 1977, we were blessed with three beautiful girls. Bihar was not the ideal place to bring up girls. A short stint at Jamalpur on deputation convinced me of this. I saw how Jamalpur, once a model, very livable railway town, had changed for the worse. Lawlessness and crime were rampant. Kidnapping, dacoities and murders were taking place within the railway premises. It was time to leave.

In August '78, by an inter-zonal transfer, I was posted as Senior Chargeman (Junior Engineer) in the Diesel Shed at Waltair/Vizag, which housed 200 locomotives and was one of the busiest sheds in the Indian Railways.

By opting for this transfer, I forfeited ten years of seniority. Prophets of doom predicted a bleak future for me, career-wise. However, the domestic scene was rosier with our three girls excelling in studies and Sheila getting on as a librarian in the school they studied at.

Honouring the First Citizen of the Republic President Dr. Rajendra Prasad at Waltair Railway Station (1954) Station Master George H. Bourne at Extreme Left

Photo courtesy: Edmund Bourne (Melbourne)

The large Anglo-Indian railway families of the '50s and '60s, the Bournes, Station Master George and his wife Teresa (née Freese), the Baxters, Chief Train Examiner Pat and Theresa with their 18 children and later the Strongs, Loco Inspector John, his wife Doreen and family had left for greener pastures.

In Vizag, there were not many Anglo-Indian railway employees – only a few drivers, fitters and cleaners, and a train guard or two. The rest were employed in the Port, the Shipyard, the Refinery, other public sector/semi-public sector organisations and the Merchant Navy.

I was the only Anglo-Indian supervisor in a group of 50 or more, but my "Anglo-Indianess" was never a liability. I was singled out for special assignments and commended several times for meritorious service.

The Bourne Family, Waltair
Back row L to R: Edmund, Trevor, George, Sylvia, Bertram, Harold, John
Seated L to R: Mom Teresa, baby Hubert, George H. Bourne
Floor L to R: Frederick, Margaret, Judaline, Valerie
Absent: Rudolph, Dorothy and Cynthia

Photo courtesy: Edmund Bourne (Melbourne)

In 1990, I was selected as Assistant Mechanical Engineer (AME) in an Open Selection on Merit Basis – a quantum career jump, a double promotion. I was posted at Bondamunda (not a bad word - literally it means "small boy's head"), a large railway complex next to Rourkela Steel City. Thus, in about twelve years, I had regained all the seniority I had lost initially.

My divisional headquarters was Chakradarpur (CKP), a one-time Anglo- Indian bastion. I had heard a lot about CKP in my boyhood – tales of guts and glory, fun and frolic, of Anglo-Indian heroes like driver Percy Carroll, and famous sportsmen – Olympian Mervyn "Bunnoo" Sutton, boxers Melville Hastings, Dougie Fernandez, Ronnie Sampayo, the Smith brothers Melvin and Owen, Philip Bibee and many others.

The CKP I visited in 1991 was a ghost town. There was a fete in the Church that Sunday. All the stalls were run by Adivasis and all the announcements were in Hindi. I came across only one Anglo-Indian, Mr. Bannister, a retired loco inspector.

Cyril Pereira, now a sprightly 94-year-old, and the oldest Anglo-Indian in Vizag, joined the Vizag Port Railways (affiliated to the B.N.R.) as a gate clerk in 1934, on a salary of Rs. 35 per month; he retired as Assistant Operating Superintendent, Waltair, Vizag, in 1970. He was posted at CKP as Section Controller from 1937 to 1946. He still remembers those halcyon days when the Anglo-Indians ruled the roost in this tiny railway town located in the tribal belt of Bihar. The majority of them left in the '50s. Today, there's no one left to tell the tale...

Let's move on to the brighter side of railway life. "What's in a name?" asked the Bard of Avon, much ahead of his time, of course. It was a typist's error, not a magic wand, that transformed my double-Irish AI friend Malcolm Murphy (his mother was a Magee) into an orthodox South Indian Brahmin.

The Baxter Railway Family of Waltair:
Back Row : (L to R) Derek, Kevon, Joan, Mary, Peter, Isabel and Sabrina
Front Row : (L to R) Bernadine, Charmaine, Terence, Mrs. Theresa Baxter, Mr. Pat Baxter, Judy, Rudolph and Anne

Photo courtesy: Sabrina Baxter

At Madras Central, Malcolm saw his name written as M.J. Murthy and with his persuasive use of Tamlish (Tamil + English) got the reservation clerk to rewrite it correctly as M.J. Murphy. All over and done with? Not quite! There was a change of shift, change of staff – another clerk came, looked at the chart. "What is this – Moorf, Moorfy?" he asked, and with a few deft strokes of his pen, restored the status quo ante. Malcolm, a good writer and full of wit himself, saw the funny side of it and decided to leave bad enough alone.

Sometimes a name is misunderstood and becomes a bone of contention. In the early fifties, a young officer walked up to the locomotive of the Calcutta-bound Mail at Waltair station and asked the driver: "Who's the guard of the train?"

"Driver, Sir," replied the Anglo-Indian driver.

"Yes, I know, but who's the guard?"

"I told you, Driver, Sir," said the grizzled veteran, obviously enjoying the greenhorn's discomfiture.

The officer was annoyed and a hot exchange followed, terminated by the timely intervention of Station Master Bourne who told the young executive: "Mr. Driver is the guard of the train."

Mr. Percy Driver's son, Jimmy was my senior in Vizag high school.

Anglo-Indian railwaymen were invariably jolly, fun-loving and humorous. Their cheerful outlook, even under pressure, took much of the drabness and drudgery out of railway work.

A PWI told me how once an Anglo-Indian driver's sense of humour bailed him out of a serious situation.

The PWI was foot-plating with his boss, the Sr. Divisional Engineer (Track) on a bad stretch of track. There was a lot of bouncing, lurching, swaying – heavy oscillation. The Sr. Engineer was furiously chastising the PWI for the poor track condition. At the first stop, he asked the driver, "How do you feel driving on a track like this?"

"Shake, rattle and roll, Sir!" replied the Anglo-Indian driver, Edgar Benjamin. The officer's anger turned to laughter – a volatile situation was defused and the PWI was lucky to get off with a warning.

Anglo-Indian drivers were noted for maintaining punctuality, and making up time, without compromising on safety.

One day, I was traveling by an express train to Vizag. The train had lost an hour or so at Kharagpur. A co-passenger had to catch a connecting flight at Vizag. I heard him anxiously ask the conductor if there was any chance of the train reaching Vizag on time.

The conductor was pessimistic, saying that drivers are wary of making up time since their "running" was under the scrutiny of speed recorders, tachograph charts, and other gadgets. Finally we arrived at Vizag. The passenger looked at his watch and exclaimed excitedly: "The train is on time, after all!"

"Yes, Sir," said the conductor. "The driver ran very well and made up for the lost time."

"He must be an Anglo-Indian!" said the passenger as he moved out of the compartment.

Anglo-Indian railway family members, wives, sons and daughters too, were familiar with railway terms, railway jargon, and some technical aspects as well; perhaps some had railway skills in their genes! Works Manager, Kharagpur, Arthur Mitchell's favourite chastisement of slip-shod work was: "My daughter could do better than that!"

Family members were inclined to use their "railway knowledge" to rise to the occasion – at times a little too high!

Mr. "M" was the Engineer-in-charge of the new diesel shed at Kharagpur. There were so many teething problems that he opted to live in the shed with his wife.

A major problem was the failure of turbochargers. Mrs. M often overheard her husband listening to the shed supervisor's report of "thick black exhaust, charge air pressure dropping, loco unable to haul the train" – typical symptoms of a turbocharger failure.

Mr. M came to the room late one afternoon, thoroughly exhausted, had his lunch, then told his wife, "I'm very tired, I'm going to sleep. Don't wake me unless it's really important."

Half an hour later the phone rang. It was the shed supervisor. A locomotive had come dead after failure. He wanted advice from the 'Sahib'.

"Hold on!" said Mrs. M. She checked on her husband who was in deep sleep. She lifted the phone and said, "Sahib wants to know what the driver reported."

"Thick black exhaust, charge air pressure zero, loco unable to haul the train," said the shed supervisor.

"Hold on!" said Mrs. M. She had heard all this before, knew it by heart. Pausing for a couple of minutes, she lifted the phone once more and told the supervisor, "Sahib bola, turbo change karo!" (Sahib said to change the turbocharger). She told Mr. M when he awoke hours later. "You should have woken me up," he said, "but you could be right." As things turned out, she was right!

It is generally believed that railway workers in the South are more disciplined and therefore, easier to manage than their northern brethren. The northern workforce is certainly more vocal, demonstrative and belligerent at times. However the southern mazdoors have their own novel, non-violent but effective "Gandhian" methods of stating their case and getting their grievance redressed.

In a division of the Southern Railway, an administrative lapse resulted in the station staff receiving only one half of their new uniforms – the top half which was a white bush coat. The bottom half, white trousers, was not supplied. The local administration was indifferent to the complaints and bluntly told the staff to wear their new bush coats over the old trousers. The staff union declared a deadline – the management remained unconcerned, till one morning the railway officers and passengers were shocked to see the station staff turned out for duty in new, starched bush coats worn over their underwear. Need I say that the trousers were supplied expeditiously, on top priority.

In the last phase of my service, I was witness to a sad but historic event – the eclipse of the good old steam locomotive. Today the steam locomotive is as dead as the dodo, but those hoary tales of guts and gore will become the stuff of ballad and legend.

Not for nothing was the steam loco called the Iron Horse. With his peak cap, half sitting, half leaning forward on the back-box, the driver was more like a jockey riding a horse, stroking its flanks and spurring it on to greater achievement. The admission and expansion of steam was controlled by positioning the lever in the driver's cab. This was connected to the valve gear and operated through a long rod aptly called the "bridle" rod. One of the motion parts was called the "stirrup" link.

It would be extremely unfair to compare the ancient steam locomotive with the latest state-of-the-art, console operated, eco-friendly diesel and electric locomotives. However, unlike the robust steam locomotive, the diesel and electric locos are so sophisticated that they have a certain "touch-me-not" quality which restricts the driver's trouble-shooting role.

Errol Peters, retired Loco Foreman of Mughalsarai, easily the biggest railway yard, related this incident to me:

While approaching Jhahjha, the end of its run, the WP locomotive hauling the Toofan Express started losing steam. There was a heavy steam blow and link motion parts on one side of the loco started falling off, one by one. The Anglo-Indian driver carried on working, confident that with one side working satisfactorily, he could roll into Jhahjha station, where the locomotive would be changed as per link.

The train was entering the station limits when a passenger in the first bogie, alarmed at the heavy leakage of steam and the sound of falling motion parts, pulled the alarm chain. The train came to a stop and couldn't be started again.

The driver was furious. He got down from the locomotive, walked up to the first bogie, noted the name of the passenger who pulled the chain and told him, "You are responsible for the failure!"

It used to puzzle me why this macho machine, the dark handsome Iron Horse, was always spoken of in the feminine gender: "She runs well, she's a beauty!" Was it because of the "petticoat", an engine part in the smoke-box, so named because of its shape? There was nothing feminine about it.

Compared to the sleek, stream-lined, garishly painted, "sexed up" effeminate looking diesel and electric locomotives, the steam locomotive was masculine to the core. Why then was it called "she"?

The question was debated a long time ago, in those railway running-rooms by drivers who put their feet up, relaxing after a long gruelling trip, and thinking about their wives and children, many miles away.

So, why was the steam locomotive called "she"? I'm sure the old steam hands, even the steam wives and daughters, will appreciate the answer and explain it to the 'uninitiated': "Because she has a tender behind!"

Percy Carroll
Anglo-Indian Hero

Francis H. McGauley, S.J.

Standing room only is the order of the day on India's trains – and a crash means more dead.

Percy D. Carroll lived a life of sacrifice and he died a life of heroic sacrifice. A lanky soft-spoken man with a quick smile and Gary Cooper ruggedness, Percy Carroll had risen to "the top" of his profession on the Railway as Driver of the Bombay-Calcutta Mail. At 49 he was well set for life with a comfortable home in Chakradharpur where he and his wife and two younger school-going children resided. Of his six children the eldest boy had gone to study for the Jesuit priesthood, two girls were working and another married.

Driver Carroll was respected for his devotion to duty despite his exacting orders at work, because he was first of all demanding of himself. He suffered through a lifetime of sickness and operations, but he was always pushing ahead. His Jesuit son, Arthur, remembers him saying, "God has asked me for a life of sacrifice, I'll give it" – and he gave it cheerfully.

Brave Heart: Beside the Engine he loved

On March 20th in the early morning hours after midnight, Driver Carroll was just picking up high speed beyond Chakradharpur's outer signal with 2 UP Bombay Mail steam locomotive when a Diesel Goods train rammed another stationary Goods train on the opposite track and sent wagons careening onto the track path of the onrushing Mail train. The Mail had received "all clear" signals ahead and there was no time for warnings. After passing the front diesel engine on the bend, suddenly Driver Carroll sighted the obstructed track at the rear. He pulled the brakes with terrible force, but he saw that a collision was imminent. He called to his firemen: "Jump for your lives; I'll save the train!" He could have jumped and saved his own life, but he thought of the hundreds of lives behind him in the train. The speed had been lessened but the crash sent the engine wildly off the tracks and spilling over the embankment. The wheels of the first car were derailed, but the train held the tracks with a shudder.

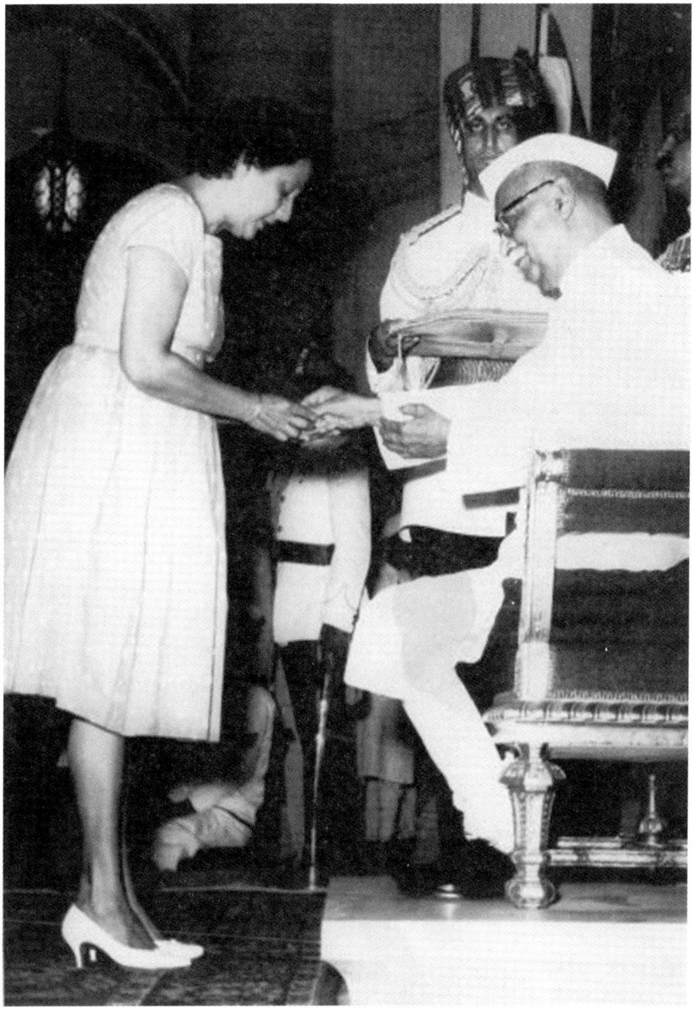

Mrs. Edna Carroll receiving the Ashoka Chakra Class II awarded posthumously to her husband, Percy Carroll from Dr. Rajendra Prasad, President of India.

Photographs courtesy: Ron & Patricia Forbes (Toronto)

Views of the Accident Site

Photographs courtesy: Ron & Patricia Forbes (Toronto)

Driver Carroll had saved hundreds of lives, but he himself lay pinned beneath his own engine. The first rescuers tried to pull him out, but his leg was crushed beneath the twisted steel. Only the water gushing out from the boiler loosened the dirt and enabled helpers to dig him out. A lady doctor from the Sind who had just returned from surgeon's training in the U.S.A. was called from the train to apply a tourniquet and give immediate treatment which prevented death at the spot.

Fortified by the Sacraments, Percy Carroll put up a courageous fight for life, but even to the end he was unselfish in his dying thoughts and inquiries about the passengers. When assured that no one had been killed (18 were injured) he spoke to those at his bedside, "I never got on the train without a prayer to Our Lady. She took care of them."

He prayed the Rosary daily and he prayed his last Rosary together with those around his bedside, as he weakly formed the Our Fathers and Hail Marys with his lips while holding the silver Rosary in his hands until his dying gasp . . . the same Rosary that was in his torn and bleeding pocket at the accident.

News of the heroic act spread quickly. First passengers from the 12-hour delayed Mail train had streamed to the hospital to inquire of, pray for, and pay their respects to the man who saved their lives. Children stood outside the hospital on their way from school where they had heard of Driver Carroll's noble act and they had hero worship in their eyes. Rickshaw wallahs, clerks and officials came in steady numbers to see the dying man.

Christ had said: "Greater love than this no man hath, that a man lay down his life for his friends."

Even those of Chakradharpur who have never heard of Christ or his words, understood it in the heroism of Percy Carroll.

* * *

Beyond the call of Duty

(Excerpt from "Britain's Betrayal in India" by Frank Anthony)

Hundreds of Anglo-Indian railwaymen have, since the founding of the railways, literally given their lives in the line of duty. On the 20th March 1959 Caroll was the driver of the Up Bombay Mail. The Mail had been given the all clear signal. Suddenly Carroll sighted an obstruction on the track. In a split second reaction he jammed the brakes, saving the lives of his crew and hundreds of passengers, sacrificing his own. He died on 22nd March 1959.

In recognition of Carroll's heroism and devotion to duty, his widow accepted the Posthumous Award of the Ashoka Chakra Class II. In addition, the Railway Administration made a special contribution to his provident fund.

Mrs. Edna Carroll wrote: "Percy joined the Railway in 1929. Three years ago, he was offered a Loco Inspector's post but he refused, saying I love my engine and I will never give up driving. I often told him, 'You work too hard and you will die on that engine'. Little did I think that my words would come true. May God rest his soul in peace."

Percy Carroll's Final Run

Noel Thomas

Percy Carroll was a brave railwayman,
He loved his engine, kept it spick and span,
He followed the Bible, prayed the Rosary,
He lived happily with family in CKP,
In the railway colony of CKP.

Percy Carroll drove the Bombay Mail,
He knew the section right from head to tail,
His firemen loved him – he treated them well,
A big-hearted driver more than words can tell.

On that tragic morning, he was driving the train
Over miles of track on the Bihar plain;
He was running to time and the signal was clear,
He had his hand on the throttle without any fear.

As the big locomotive came round the bend,
Percy was certain that his life would end;
His sole concern was how to save the train,
And hundreds of travellers – he couldn't die in vain,
The brave engine driver wouldn't die in vain.

He eased the throttle and applied the brakes,
He knew he would crash into the fouling rakes,
He yelled to his firemen, "Save yourselves, Jump!"
And along with his engine, he went over the hump.

The rest of the train had stopped and was still,
With no one injured due to Percy's skill,
They couldn't save him though they tried their best,
The good Lord called Percy to eternal rest.

These were his last words, "Has anyone died?"
He smiled on hearing that all had survived,
His life had ended, his race was won,
When Percy Carroll made his final run.

Just the way it was...

Eugene D'Cruz

I was born on the 11th November 1921 to Anthony and Lucy D'Cruz (née D'Rosario) in Gooty, a small remote railway colony about mid-way, on the Madras to Bombay railway line.

My granddad was in the railway service in the mid-1880s as a Surveyor on the Londa to Goa line of the West India Portuguese Railway when tunnels were being built, and the Railway operated by the staff of the old Southern Maharatta Railway. He was later absorbed as a railway guard, stationed in Belgaum, working trains north to Miraj and Poona and south to Castle Rock and Goa. Sometime in 1908, he was transferred to Gooty. At this time The Southern Maharatta Railway and The Madras Railway were amalgamated to form the Madras and Southern Maharatta Railway. Granddad served in Gooty till 1924 and retired as a mail guard. At this time in 1918, the Asian flu struck Gooty. My grandma, three aunts and an uncle among many others died; it was very tragic.

My father after serving in Iraq during WWI was posted to Gooty in the Mechanical Department where he met and married my mother in 1921.

Gooty was a railway colony and the town itself was about 3 miles away and boasts of a fine Tippu Sultan Fort with ramparts and towering walls, which at one time had British troops and a hospital. When I was a young lad, Gooty was a small colony, with about 30 Anglo-Indian families and other communities, a dispensary, a wee Railway School for Anglo-Indian kids, a Railway Institute and it was a one street town. A road ran alongside the tracks with a row of houses and at the back of those boulder strewn hills, went deep inland. On the other side of the tracks were more houses for the traffic and lower cadre staff, the railway station, locomotive shed and an armoury that stored the weapons of the Auxiliary Force, the paramilitary wing of the British Indian Army which every Anglo-Indian railwayman had to join. Beyond a boundary wall lay the small village, the beautiful Catholic Church of St. Joseph's, served by the Dutch Mill Hill Fathers, a place that strengthened our faith and made the community a close knit family. A few shops, bakery, a general store owned by Mr. Merawanjee, a Parsi gentleman, and a post office and beyond that wild country.

It was an interesting place, a range of rock strewn hills, fields of ground nut, paddy, cholam, ragi and other grains that grow in arid places. There were a number of lakes with wild game and migratory birds. The surrounding hills teemed with wild life, panthers, black and spotted deer, wild boar, hyenas, jackals, wild rabbit (hare) and a variety of snakes, both in species and size, that were attracted by home gardens and poultry. I was told that nearly every family had guns for small game; a few like Mr. Paddy Burke, a driver and an ex-Army man who was also the Staff Sergeant Instructor for the Station's Auxiliary Force, had a rifle for big game.

Salaries were small before and during the depression; it was frugal living, and as the saying goes – what you don't see or hear you won't miss. English veggies as we called cabbage, carrots and the like did not grow there. We had them once a year when our general merchant Mr. Merawanjee went to Bangalore and did our Christmas shopping... every family gave him a list, and nearly everyone wanted salt beef, ham and bacon. We had to do with small fresh water fish and sometimes Mr. Burke on his trips with the slow goods train would take his gun and get a black buck that grazed like cattle in the black cotton fields. The generous man would share it with the folks around. With no electricity and no fridges, the venison was cured, dried and made into ding-ding – we kids simply loved the salted meat.

There were no cinema houses or radios in those days. Only one newspaper that came every morning by the Madras Mail; we had a stack of old magazines sent from England, a circulating library... enough to keep us kids happy and excited. We had caring teachers and a lot of old nanas watched us like hawks. It was a rule that wherever we went the girls had to be with us whether we liked it or not. Dare they be left out they'd scream "Nana"!!!

In those days, most homes had either a piano, a violin, banjo, accordion, flute or mandolin. The pianists played the latest songs thanks to the music books they got regularly from England.

When one couldn't afford a daily nip of Scotch, the Lambadis (a famous nomadic tribe) would supply the thirsty with hell fire grog, hidden in tapered bundles of firewood. I loved their mournful songs; probably it was the story of their hard lives and their distant past.

Try to imagine this scene: a silent street lit with kerosene lamps, lined with huge fig trees, dimly lit homes, lit by petromax lamps, and then hear the beautiful music of someone playing the piano or the flute, the singing with a banjo, that was indeed music, to remember, to dream, to take you back to days gone by.

The President's Special – Bangalore Cantonment - 1961
L to R: ___, M. Peters, _____, H. D'Rosario, _______, L.G. Pacheco,
E.R. D'Cruz, Max Gaughan, ___, ____, Mr. Lopez

Photo courtesy: Eugene D'Cruz (Sydney)

The memory of our Institute dances that were held periodically and at Christmas time remains vivid in mind. We kids were allowed at dances that lasted till near morn. We could not be left alone in those big widely spaced homes; we hung around doors, around the band or had our own fun on the verandah that circled the Institute. I still cannot believe the grandeur: every gent in a suit, some ex-Army men in shell jackets, waxed whiskers... I am writing about the mid and late years of 1920s... dancing pumps, dangling watch chains with pendants and gloves on the right hand. Every lady in a long gown, well-bedecked and ready for the Waltz, Roger De Coverly, the Grand March and Lancers, a dance that's fascinating, the movements, the weaving and all the curtseying, the galloping Polka, the Charleston and all the then latest steps. How and where did those bucks learn those fancy steps? The

Anglo-Indian flair? Going through some instructions from dance mags? Whatever, it was a vision straight out of scenes from *The Great Gatsby*. The courtesy of thanking a lady after the dance, and what would she like? "Port and Lemon" was the favourite. The gents prefered whiskey and soda or gin and ginger, a combination that now seems odd.

Driver Eugene D'Cruz

We went to a small Railway School for Anglo-Indians. It was just s primary school with a batch of about 8 boys and 6 girls. Strange to say all of us remained lifelong friends; an uncanny bond kept us in touch. By the third standard we had to go to boarding schools, as there were no English schools close by... most of the boys went to St. Joseph's Bangalore, just two to Madras and the girls to St. Philomena's Bellary, which was a garrison town, a night's journey away.

In time the girls married. Most of the boys joined the railways and scattered but met often in running rooms or at weddings. I started as an apprentice fireman in Hubli, and then to my delight was transferred to Gooty my home town, but it was short lived. An inspecting loco officer, a Parsi and fatherly bloke, saw me and knowing that my dad was a chargeman in the loco shed at Arkonam, said I was too young and foot loose (I was 19) and had to be with my parents. The next day I was transferred to Arakonam, a place and colony I did not like. At this time World War II was raging in Europe and Africa and there was a drive to enlist railwaymen to serve in the Armed Forces. As an aside, when I joined the Railways like all other Anglo-Indians, I had to enlist in the Railway regiment of the AF (I).

To my astonishment, within a week I was released from railway duties and sent to a training camp in Jalandhar. Within five months of Army training we were shipped out via Karachi to Basra and in a short time assigned to a loco shed to operate and manage the train service in conjunction with the Iraqi State Railways.

It was four and a half years of working in the desert, living in tents, under extreme weather conditions and sand storms. On the bright side, we had an opportunity to go to Beirut, Damascus and visit the Holy Land. We made it to the end of the War with no regrets. Maybe we missed out on family, social life, comforts of a home, but we made lifelong friends, learnt patience, strict discipline and above all to accept whatever life dished out to us, the good and the bad.

After the war, we went back to our old jobs and due promotions were given. I was posted back to Arakonam, where I met my wife Audrey Brass. She was the daughter of a retired driver, with two sisters teaching in the local railway school and an aunt who was a railway hospital nurse, and other relatives in various departments of the Railway; indeed, a railway family like mine.

Years went by getting promotions, from a fireman to a goods train driver, passenger driver, a mail driver to a special grade on super-fast services... enjoying the comradeship of a unique breed The Running Staff... some of whom were legends and some with unique characters. We had our ups and downs, share of sickness in the family and the passing of an older generation. Co-workers now with bigger families worrying about their schooling, their time in boarding schools (the Arakonam Railway School was only until standard 8 and so we had to send our children away to boarding schools to finish their education).

39 years and 8 months later, I retired, shall I say I was a survivor? I loved my railway life, my co-workers, my colony, and all the things, good and bad that came my way. I raised six boys and one girl, saw them all married and they presented us with 13 grandchildren. Sadly my wife of over 40 years passed away in 1990. With all my children having migrated to Australia and no relatives left in India (except for one niece), I joined my family in Australia. I now live in Sydney with my daughter and her family. I visit my four sons in Melbourne and two in Perth every year. In fact, three of my sons are following the family tradition and are drivers in Melbourne. They are the fourth generation of railwaymen in my family serving from the mid-1880s.

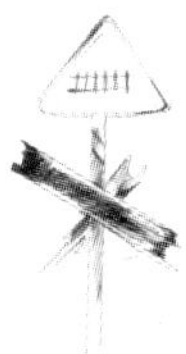

Asansol
The Golden Glow of the Past

Philip Boezalt

On the Railways there were several grades for Drivers. There were the Covenanted Drivers, who were British and who received their salaries in pounds sterling, a part of which was remitted to their bank accounts in Britain. Not highly educated, but highly competent. They felt the snag in the engine in their very bones, much like the conductor of an orchestra who feels a false note in his body. Most of them were quite generous to their staff, gentle but strict. An order was an order. "Carry out orders first and appeal later" was the slogan of the time. In this way, discipline was always at its highest.

There was next, the "Co-ordinate" scale of pay which was less than the above-mentioned. It was in this scale that the Anglo-Indians were employed. It was a good scale and the drivers were comfortable on this. Overtime and work on Sundays added to their pay packet. These men lived very well having well-kept homes and plenty on the table. They kept three to four servants and sent their children to very good schools in the hills and in Asansol. At that time there was the Railway School for the Railway children only, and "Oak Grove" in Jharanpani, Mussoorie.

Later there came the new scale of pay which was jokingly called the Japanese scale; later other pay scales came in monitored by Pay Commissions.

Durand Institute at Asansol, built in 1878

In the days gone by, every house had a well-kept compound bordered by a hedge, which was trimmed by a mali supplied by the Inspector of Works (IOW). There was keen competition, and no pain or expense was spared in the upkeep of the garden. At the end of the year the Divisional Superintendent awarded prizes for the best kept garden and individual prizes for the best roses, dahlias and other flowers.

Sports activities were encouraged. Most of the men who brought glory in the field of sports in the Olympics were railwaymen. The railway officers encouraged the workmen and were often seen on the fields watching the matches and encouraging the athletes.

The Anglo-Indians were a fun-loving community. We had the Durand Institute for dances, housie and other entertainment. This Institute was founded in the year 1878 within the

European Colony of Asansol and was called the European Institute. In 1925, it was renamed as the Durand Institute after Sir Mortimer Durand.

We had our annual Christmas festivities starting from 24th December. People visited their neighbours and friends and there was the offering of the famous "Burra Din" cake and sweets and not to forget some little wine and a shot of rum and whisky for good cheer. Thirty-first December was always a night to remember because of the big dance to bring in the New Year.

A few members of the Anglo-Indian community at Asansol. Philip Boezalt is seen at the back.

Work in those days was a pleasure, as each driver had his own permanent locomotive which he and his staff looked after as if it were their own private possession. The drivers spent a lot of their own money keeping the locomotive sparklingly clean. They applied fresh coats of paint and polished brass and copper with great fondness. Some drivers would go to the length of being fanatics and visit "Vishwanath Gully" in Benaras to buy or order decorative parts for the locomotives. These shops supplied hand signal lamps for the guards and decorations for the driver's engines. Devotion to duty was also an outstanding feature of a section of running staff. During the strike by the loco staff in 1974, a large number of Anglo-Indian drivers reported for duty and kept the trains moving from Howrah to Mughalsarai under terrible hardships.

There is a saying that "behind every great man there is a woman". The wives of the running staff were indeed the unsung heroines. Night after night at any hour these faithful women saw their husbands off to duty and again greeted them at any hour with a hot meal. Many of them even signed the Call Book to allow their men a few more minutes of sleep. Every driver had his individual code whistle, which he gave to let the wife know that he was now on his way out and on return for her to put the kettle on.

The railways provided the Missionaries with plots of land for building schools. This was at the time of the British Raj when the officers were British and the sub-ordinates Anglo-Indians or Indians. Here, as in the running of the railway, there was discipline and commitment.

For the benefit of the Christians, land was given and various facilities were also provided. There were several denominations of Christians, the Catholic Church of the Sacred Heart, The Anglican Church and the Methodist Chapel. To cater to the various domestic needs of the people, the market came up. Besides shops run by Indians, there were some run by Jews and Armenians. The markets and the roads were kept very clean. There was just one police town Sergeant, whom everybody feared. He usually was a military man, and there was perfect law and order.

To provide medical attention for the railwaymen and families, the Railway Hospital was built. For the women there was the Burlington Hospital which took care of maternity cases and other ailments. Later everything was shifted to the new Railway Hospital and the old place was converted into quarters for nurses.

The railway colony was divided into loco and traffic quarters and later medical quarters for the medicos. The traffic quarters were for those who dealt with traffic and also commercial staff. Here again cleanliness and order was the watch word of the day.

Such were my days. Let the present generation speak for itself.

Photographs courtesy: The Boezalt family

Bitragunta
Gone are the days!

Marlene Powell

Bitragunta is a station on the Delhi-Madras Grand Trunk Route, between Kavali and Nellore, a few train hours away from Chennai. My Dad was a driver there, my Mom a homemaker. We were two sisters and three brothers, a happy railway family of boiler makers, train examiners, electricians with the exception of myself, an office superintendent.

Bitragunta was a hub of Anglo-Indian culture. Its pride was the "Home of the Steel Horses", they called the round house loco shed with WPs, WMs, etc., meticulously maintained by chargemen like Gilbert, Walter, and Eardley Moreira and Vernon Faraday under efficient foremen like Noel Bush and Rozario.

I remember engine drivers such as Robby Trutwein, Sunna Mitchell, Rabel, Tita Wrightman and Arthur Morgan, officers Mr. Green and Mr. Ringrow, auditors Soans and Popley, station superintendent Fertnig, guards Roberts and Blakey.

The old European and Anglo-Indian Institute was the epicenter of entertainment. Willie Gordon would organize the dances and start the ball rolling with his signature tune: 'Red Sails in the Sunset'. Young men and pretty maids would shake a leg. With Offee Magee emceeing the show, no one dared to go overboard even with "dutch courage". Offee would persuade them to leave, sometimes not so gently, but using his famous left hook only as a last resort. The receiver was picked up from the bushes early next morning. Offee, a driver, was the railways boxing champion in his weight. Bitragunta had its own band, with Violet Roberts on the piano, Pat and Alfie D'Silva on the violin, Vernon Lamb and Rendell Roberts.

The Railway School, ably managed by Mrs. May Bird (Head Mistress), got cent per cent results for 13 years. Except for vernacular language teachers, all others were Anglo-Indians, Georgina Abrew, May Magee and Mina Day to name a few. They encouraged us to study well, to aim high and to entertain ourselves and others with contests, picnics, sports and dinners.

Home of Steel Horses, Round House, Bitragunta

Photo courtesy: Marlene Powell

There were two Dutch priests in charge of the Holy Family Church. They trained our choir, consisting of May and Rita D'Silva, Averil Moreira, Barbara Managan, Celine Martinz, Colleen Gordon and organist Violet Roberts.

No more Bitragunta with the huge bungalows, the sprawling compounds, the lovely gardens; no more cow-heel and dosa by Cruze Mary; no more hoppers and puli fry and puffs by Yankata, or boti curry from those ayahs, or grog from the lady who sold it. Gone are the days and the good old Bitraguntans who once lived in this railway town.

Cheers and bladders down the hatch!

Bhusawal
Sweet Memories

Doreen Fritchley-Aranha

When I saw the painting on the cover of *Anglos In The Wind* by Anglo-Indian artist Raymond D'Monte of two small children waving at a passing train hauled by a steam engine, the scene took me back in time to my childhood years in my hometown, Bhusawal.

My father, Gerald Fritchley, was a mail driver on the good old GIPR. He had his own special 'Bullet' steam engine and his assigned crew – fireman Sam Conley, a young Jewish lad who married Lovina Austen and eventually settled in Israel, and Augwalla Mehndi, a Muslim. While we lived in 40 Blocks, we usually took an evening stroll to the White Gate – the level crossing at 10 Blocks – and waved to all the drivers whose trains passed by. Each one had a special whistle by which the family members knew of their arrival or departure.

My father and mother (Alberta O'Neill) had 11 children. We initially lived in 12 Blocks until my father accepted a 3-year transfer to Igatpuri. But our family loved Bhusawal so much that after our return to 40 Blocks in 1944, he refused transfers to Itarsi, Nagpur and Jhansi at our behest.

Although the official railway Institute, called the Senior

Institute, was located near the officers' quarters at 6 Blocks, most of our social life centered around the little Limpus Club at 40 Blocks. I do remember when the Second World War ended, we had a celebration at the Senior Institute and a cut-out of Adolph Hitler was used as an Aunt Sally and we children had a whale of a time trying to aim a tennis ball through his open mouth. The Senior Institute was also the venue for dances when railway teams from Mhow, Ratlam, etc., would come down to play hockey and football matches on the huge *maidan* nearby.

Standing L to R: Gwen Pritchard, Mrs. Evans, Patsy O'Leary, Teresa O'Leary, Tom Evans, Maureen Orchard, Elaine Chappell, Merlin Rose, Margaret Evans, (?) (?) and Thelma Woodman
Kneeling L to R: Ken Pritchard, Lionel Dexter, Hazel Simmons, Doreen, Fritchley, Lorna Jones, Mignon Owers, Elaine Orchard, Joyce Evans, Norma Jones and Mavis Evans
Sitting L to R: Peter Woodman, Doreen O'Leary and Rudy Woodman

The babu in charge of the Club was Chote Lal – initially he and I were 'enemies' as I had the habit of visiting the reading room to read the London Illustrated and Daily Mirror when no one else was around and I would place my small dog, Buttons, on his chair. However, we eventually became great friends. He was very popular with all the members and some, even when they migrated, kept in touch with him. We would have friendly matches – netball and tennequoit – with the residents of 12 Blocks and Guards Line. But most of all, I recall our lovely Christmas celebrations. Like all railway colonies it was a 10-day affair, the most notable events being the pagal sports. We'd have a donkey race with the jockeys seated backwards, running to a bench with our hands tied behind and slurping cold drinks from a saucer and then running to the finishing line with it in our mouths. Also leaping up at buns loaded with honey suspended just out of reach and since our hands were tied for this event too, every time we jumped to take a bite, we'd get absolutely gooey in the process. We'd have cockfights in sacks – the last one standing being the winner.

Standing L to R: Saucy Murray, Una Thompson, Althea Brown, Jessie Gurr, M. Jingell, Trevor Fritchley, Winnie Allen, Mrs. Green, Doris Bent
Sitting L to R: Beryl & Olga Fritchley, Cuchoo Murray, (?) and Eunice White

We had British and American troops posted in Bhusawal during the war years and I remember our Anglo-Indian boys objecting to their dancing with our girls and starting a fracas in the process. But we children who had to walk to the Railway School at 12 Blocks loved it when the soldiers would stop their trucks and give us a lift. A family named Green owned a bullock cart and their children and a few others got to ride to school in it. The only other transport was a tonga owned by Mehtab who lived in the Allen family's outhouse. Here again only a few children could be accommodated and we unlucky ones would chase after it and jump on the iron rod behind and Mehtab would flick his whip backwards to discourage us from hanging on.

We had only the Railway School, so after Standard 4 everyone had to go to boarding school; La Martiniere, Lucknow, or Barnes High School, Deolali.

Since 40 Blocks was a great distance from the railway station, church and market, we'd take a short cut through the railway shed and sometimes wangle a ride on the pilot engine. As we got older we'd ride our bicycles around and under Satara Bridge or carry them over the railway bridge to reach the market on the other side.

We had only one theatre, The Linda, showing English movies once a week. The Anglo-Indian girls in Bhusawal were really pretty and the locals would line up on the street leading to the theatre, to watch them go by. Our May Queen Balls were well-attended and our first May Queen was Marie Shaw. Others I recall were Margaret Hassett, Mary Hall, Eileen Blanchette and Pamela Wilson and, of course, Diana Valentine, who became Miss India.

Incidentally, my Uncle Bertie's family were accomplished musicians and Fritchley's Band was well-known for providing good dance music not only in Bhusawal but other neighbouring railway towns as well.

The Tapti River in those days was a lovely, clean river and we'd delight in taking walks alongside, wading in the shallows or looking down at it from the railway bridge and seeing the beautiful Satpura range of hills in the distance, which would become an ethereal purple at dusk.

Those were the days! Regretfully, in 1954, we had to leave as Dad decided to settle in England. Though I returned to stay in India, I went back to Bhusawal on just two visits in the '60s. It has changed so much now that I prefer living with my memories.

Photographs courtesy: Doreen Fritchley-Aranha

Bezawada
The Green, Green Grass of Home

Barbara James

"Home Is Where The Heart Is" and all our hearts beating as one made the railway quarters at Winchpet. Vijayawada, our home – with many beautiful memories to be cherished for the rest of our lives.

Dad (Harvey Harrison) was in the Control Office – Bezawada (fondly known as Blazewada due to the extreme summers) later renamed Vijayawada. Mum (Aileen) as in those days, kept the home fires burning.

The Winchpet Railway Colony was a huge sprawling lay-out, closed off on three sides – with well-planned quarters and fantastic open spaces to play in. When you entered the colony, the outside world almost ceased to exist. Here my brother Vernon and sisters Jennifer and Phyllis and all our friends spent many happy and carefree days.

In the backyard grew a big, majestic fig tree and later an almond tree grew next to it. Dad helped us build a tree-house amongst the fig tree branches and we spent many hours of leisure up there with our favourite comics and snacks – green mango with chillie powder, borums, kerks and of course the tasty kamarakut sweets.

Years went by – dad was transferred and we moved away, - but there was always in our hearts a strong longing to go back someday and visit the home that held so many happy memories – if it was still there.

As the years passed with careers and family this dream had to be put on hold – till one day my sister confirmed her holiday to India and the main item on her agenda was to visit Vijayawada. Thanks to her determination, both of us made the long overdue trip (it was about four decades after we left Vijayawada) which became an epic journey.

Ramgopal Choultry Arch
(before the entrance to the Vijayawada Railway Colony)

As our train crossed the Krishna River, we listened to the familiar sounds and stared out of the window in awe at many of the old still familiar sights. When we alighted from the train the modernisation with time was quite apparent, but the old over-bridge was still there – with just a facelift of widening and lengthening to accommodate the additional platforms. The Control Office and the Railway Institute that held a lot of good memories of dances and other functions from where many friendships did build up was still there (though the Institute was apparently now being used by the Union). The Railway Hospital had been expanded where quarters once existed.

In front of the Quarters – Barbara James (Centre), Vijayawada

Photographs courtesy: Barbara James

Since we had limited time, after a sumptuous lunch, we set off with our friend, who had very kindly taken a few days off to show us around. We took an auto-rickshaw and as we sped to the colony, we kept looking out eagerly for familiar locations. The entrance to the colony was just before the Ramgopal Choultry Arch (which had stood the test of time) and as our auto turned in we were filled with anticipation and excitement. But to our dismay and shock we found the well laid out quarters had been replaced with a sea of flats – some of which seemed to have been built as after thoughts – it could either be called the modern trend or more accurately a tragedy! The quarters were all cramped together with narrow winding lanes in between. We looked around aghast and totally disoriented. All that was familiar was the hill in front of us and the mosque on the other side. We tried in vain to visualise where our quarters must have stood but nothing felt right. With heavy hearts and great disappointment we were forced to leave.

Bezawada, December 1965.

Back row 2nd from right – Noel Merritt, extreme right Reggie "Killer" Francis.
1st row standing (L to R): Lossy Harper, Basil D'Menzie, Bobby Parker, Eslin Parker, Ronnie Leslie, and Mr. Andrews Station Superintendent. Seated (L to R): Mrs. Harper and Mrs. D'Menzie and others.

Photo courtesy: Brian Merritt

The rest of the day was more satisfying – a trip to the Krishna River where we had spent many of our school holidays – fishing or just sitting around on the barrage when the sluices were closed. We then went past our old church enroute to our school. One of the nuns very kindly took us around – it had expanded so much it almost looked unfamiliar. I was happy to see the old chapel which hadn't seemed to have changed and where I had spent many a quiet moment. We then drove past the old cinema theatre Leela Mahal (another place chock full of memories!) which was dwarfed by the tall modern buildings all around.

That night when going over the day's events, we decided to make one more attempt the next day – to locate our quarters – but this time on foot.

We were up early and first visited the Gandhi Hill – where a library now stood. Though it was not visiting hours, a bit of persuasion and few phone calls to the authority in charge and we were escorted by one of the security guards to the top. When we were young we had scrambled up the hill umpteen times using the shrubs and rocks to pull ourselves up, now there were roads leading up.

Though it was thrilling visiting the hill, the urge to go back to the quarters was too strong and we hurried down. We stopped the auto at the foot of the Railway bridge under the old banyan tree (which must be over 100 years old) and began walking down the old familiar road towards the quarters. This time we let our hearts and feet do the navigating down the road we had trod for almost 15 years.

At the arch we turned into the quarters – the old quarters on the right looked the same as we walked alongside them – instead of going straight ahead, as we had done the previous day, fallen away and out of force of habit our feet took a slight detour behind the first row of quarters. We stopped and looked around and just stood there silent – our hearts skipped a beat when our eyes fell on the foundation remains of a twin block. My sister and myself looked at each other in disbelief – then using the Choultry wall as a guide we began to realise that this might well be the foundation of ours and French's quarters.

We scrambled up onto what was left of the foundation and began walking around identifying each room. To be doubly sure we decided to try and find the fig tree or almond tree. We worked our way to where we thought they would be and even though the grass and weeds were overgrown we kept searching around.

Minutes later with a cry of delight I found a few almonds on the ground and as I continued to look around I struck gold – lo and behold, there were two dried figs and nearby we spotted the old fig and almond trees, their branches entwined. It seemed that both were holding on to each other and the beautiful memories of the past. Our blood ran cold – we now knew for sure we had found the remains of our home after almost forty five years.

We ran around with joy (would have danced if we could) our cameras clicking away capturing images that would always be etched in our hearts and minds. We would never know why when the rest of the colony had been demolished and rebuilt – only the foundation of this twin block had been spared. I told my sister that somebody up there knew we would be back one day and had kept it safe till such time destiny drew us back to keep our date with the past.

We stayed as long as we could walking from room to room reminiscing about the past and my sister revealed a secret she had faithfully kept all these years – pointing to the small room she said this was where my brother hid all his tuck! It was as if we could feel the presence of mum and dad. It was with heavy hearts but with a feeling of over-whelming joy and fulfillment we had to finally leave, looking back for a last farewell before we turned the bend to the main road. The experience was surreal and just being able to see and touch the green, green grass of home, for one last time was priceless!

BEYOND THE FENCE

Rebecca Taylor

MOISTURE DIFFUSED THE air and the cold mist settled as dew drops on rose petals – typical Bangalore weather. Twittering sparrows in the trees, occasional happy barking of a dog, and reverberation of the steam trains passing by, are classic examples of railway colony ambience.

Railway life was simple and yet at the heart of it all was every railway employee's universe. Those white picket fences with the vines of Morning Glory trailing over trellised houses and large compounds made up their world.

When growing up in a railway colony one couldn't help notice that every public building began with the word railway: railway school, railway hospital, railway institute and so on.

Living in the colony was more than just trains. It was really a journey of life passed on from one generation to another. Every child aspired to be a railway employee one day. It seemed like the best career option. Each morning one would wake up with the sound of the trains and this was the beginning of another day of simple railway life.

Where else could one grow up hearing the terms "box boy" or "going on line"?... I'm going down a nostalgic path thinking of those dark green trellises and looking at that wooden board nailed to it that read "Mr. Phillip Gilles", #305/C

Railway Quarters. The little board revealed to the rest of the world that this was home. It's something I looked at everyday and something I so fondly miss. My grandfather Phillip Gilles worked as a Senior Loco Inspector for the Southern Railways. He spent his childhood in Golden Rock... but soon grew accustomed to the Bangalore lifestyle, a routine he did not want to leave. He was promoted to AME but declined it to continue living in Bangalore. Philip had a love affair with the railways. He joined in 1953 and since then it was a magical train ride for him.

Illustration: Rebecca Taylor

Illustration: Rebecca Taylor

As a little girl I would take a stroll with my grandfather. He would show me the engines and the guard boxes. He would tell me stories on our way back home: how difficult it was to be a shunter, how hot the fire box was, and how one needed a strong arm to shovel coal. Memories of his stories still linger in my mind.

Was it the hustle and bustle of the station or the sound of the trains rolling in, or was it the distinctive drivers' code whistle, there was always something intriguing about the railways.

Illustration: Rebecca Taylor

As the coal dust settled, the evening beckoned us; the lights were turned on and the whole family would gather and listen to railway stories and those famous Anglo-Indian "Pat Yarns" over a meal of piping hot beef stew and bread. Later in the still of the night, you could clearly hear the last trains running through in the distance, the clackety-clack on the tracks diminishing as they sped away.

The sound to us simple railway folk was never a disturbance... it was a beautiful lullaby to our ears.

CKP Days

Denise Smith

My trip down memory lane takes me to the best of my years in CKP, Chakradharpur. We Anglo-Indians called it Chickardapur, Chicago or just CKP. I grew up there. I remember those rows of houses, homes of Anglo-Indian families with names like Bannister, Rodrigues, Green, Hogg, Godfrey, Lovery, O'Leary, Avery, Wrightman, Footman, Walker, Faulkner, Reed, Sneyd – one surname seemed to rhyme with another. CKP was one of the most happening railway colonies, a kind of anachronism in the tribal belt of Bihar.

People from Kharagpur, Bilaspur, Sini, even Calcutta came for our dances. My aunts Yvonne, Olga and Audrey Rodrigues would come down from Cal. The Black and White Ball was a famous dance. I vaguly remember grandma Phyllis taking off to Calcutta to have my Mom's and Aunts' dresses tailored there.

It was such a pleasure, just to sit back and watch some of those lovely dances – waltz, fox-trot, jive – with good dancers like Jimmy and Patsy Bannister, Tony and Coral Stiffle, James and Keki Samuels and the Walkers enjoying themselves on the dance floors. Among the younger group, the jivers Grenville and Maureen enjoying themselves on the dance floor. Stiffle, Trevor Rodrigues, Duncan Francis, Keith and Diddley O'Leary were some of the enthusiastic dancers – now I know where I learned my dancing steps.

CKP was also synonymous with boxing, local and Inter Railway Championships, with boxers from all over India in action: Neville Scott, Trevor and Perky Rordrigues, Dougie Fernandes and the Santragachi great Freddie MacMarquis. The tournament always ended with a dance. I must have been four or five years old at that time and remember clinging to my grandma Phyllis who was in charge of refreshments.

CKP and Christmas is a terrific combination! A show every day, sports, fancy dress parties, etc., from the 15th December till the 7th of January.

The Iron Bridge of CKP

Photo courtesy: William Vengeance

I remember preparing and putting up the Christmas bonfire with the Hogg sisters Betty, Sandy, Patu and Tina. Then, reaching home after Midnight Mass, we were shocked to see only the ashes of our bonfire – the Smith brothers had done their naughty needful. 36 hours of labour gone up in smoke

– we were angry then but, at the Calcutta Reunion held in 2012, we talked about it and laughed heartily. I remember the Christmas Day Jam session, the game of Rounders on the field opposite Bhola's shop.

Then, there was the Amateur Hour, which showcased promising talent like Dudley Wilson in his cowboy hat, Uncle Vanjour on the guitar and Joe Lebroy singing the 'Tennesse Waltz' – what an amazing voice! And Dougie Rodrigues doing the Tiger Dance in the freezing cold, only in paint and chuddies. Pagal Gymkhana on a mad, mad afternoon: ladies chasing a cockbird, the men chasing a feary greasy pig, and the Queen of Sheba game.

Jimmy Bannister's pound party had amazing food – 25 to 30 different home cooked dishes on display. How can I forget the favourite Iron Bridge, the hot spot of CKP, a cameraman's delight, close to our favourite picnic spot. The Iron Bridge was to CKP what Howrah Bridge was to Calcutta.

Get togethers of our younger group were spontaneous events, where boys took a notice around and collected 25 paise as an entry fee; the money would be spent on sandwiches and juices. The favourite venues were Ronny Hogg's and Joe Walker's – they had a great selection of music.

There's always a yearning to go back to my hometown. Each revisit brings back great memories and gives me a sense of feeling good. That's what CKP is all about – warmth, entertainment and bonding.

CKPites

William Vengeance

St. Martin asked Howell is D'vine and is Godfrey? The answer was Avery puzzling one. Is there a Sherzpill to transform a Mael into a Lamb? It is Sutton we will Vogt Foran Adam to come and not Leavers to Freeze in the Gale.

Harris, your Grey matter will turn to Brown and Green, even if you put your Hatton, it will make no difference. Will you Russell from Jordan to Chicago? Oh father, this is something Neu.

Now, come down to D'Brass tacks. Assume it was the Power of the prospect to leave India. They began to Reid a dismal future here. Was it Wrightman to go away, just to be like the Jones is? So be a smart Cooke and put your Nicholson in the Gillbanks. By Hasting you won't Ward off the threat. It's Hollingsworth and sons, Davidson, Thompson, Peterson, Issacson, Dawson. Succeed you Wilson, it is Taylor Maede for you. Where are the Babas and Bibees? Have a Hart, if its not a Fulton, take a Middleton or a VanHaeften. Have your Nipps in Bartles of Feegrade quality. Does this ring a Bell like Ballantyne? Frank-ly speaking, we have Eaton food, and ordinary Hogg dressed up and called slice Kingham. O'leary, anything will do except Cattamole. When on D'Cruz, don't count D'Costa, spend D'Silva as if it was D'Brass. Make it Kingsley, do your duty as per Rossiter, to overcome one Sneyd.

When old age comes, be you a Walker or Footman, you will need the support of a Bannister to reach Cloud Nine. Then you cannot Duckett. The angel sits Pentony (pen to knee) writing the Benedict.

No, don't make Fernandez (Fun of this) I'm not speaking French – my name? I'm Anglo-Indian, A-one. Vengeance is mine!

Editor's Note:
The surnames mentioned in the article belonged to Anglo-Indians who actually lived in the CKP railway colony.

Dongargarh
A Bengal-Nagpur Railway Colony

Phyllis Copcutt

The past is our history and I can recall mine as if it happened only yesterday. It was September 1949 and I was teaching part-time in Nagpur after completing my Diploma, when a vacancy occurred in a Bengal-Nagpur Railway School in Dongargarh (now in Chhattisgarh State). As it was not far from my home town, Nagpur, I applied, much to my parents' dismay as I was then just 18 years old. My boarding school mistress's words kept ringing in my ears: "Phyllis Gregory, you're a frightened goose in a dormitory; how are you going to live alone?" However, nothing could deter me. I had made my bid for independent living and I was like a bird ready for flight.

My acceptance into the job did wonders for me, after living behind the sheltered walls of a convent and teachers' college for many years. My mother was determined to accompany me and thanks to her, I settled into the triplex with two other lady teachers. It was partly furnished with a bed, cupboard, table, chairs and toilet fittings. My first home looked pretty and comfortable after displaying my books in a fancy book case. There were a few cushions, a vase of flowers and checked curtains.

Our close proximity to a big black rocky hill was quite picturesque, but folk tales of wild animals such as panthers, bears, wolves and hyenas were scary.

Since there were no sightings of wild animals we lived fearlessly, till trouble began...

There was a lone building not far from our quarters where, in earlier days, a butcher cut meat to supply the colony, but later was used by a baker who supplied us with bread, biscuits and cake, as there was no supermarket, as such. There was a vegetable and meat market outside the colony and the cooks did the shopping.

I had heard from the older residents that the panthers and hyenas would come down at night for the soup bones, and my cook woman had sworn that she saw a panther in my backyard while the hyenas continued their nocturnal roaming. One afternoon, on my return from school, a curious crowd had gathered near the hill and the drama unfolded when the panther came into view.

The local shikari who was an Anglo-Indian engine driver, was called out and they all waited until the animal was shot dead. Nobody cared whether the panther was the last of the species on the hill. The preservation of human life was obviously more important, especially us teachers. Sadly, they found two cubs which were given to the Rajah Sahib (Indian Prince) for his own private zoo. This event marked my initiation into life in Dongargarh.

It was a small colony which was always kept clean, bright and tidy, despite the lack of such modern amenities as deep sewerage, electricity and piped water. The streets and homes were lit up by gas lamps and a trusted band of servants filled water from the wells for the homes. There were two or three hydrants some distance from our house so we depended on the water carriers.

Many families, including teachers like myself, had cooks to prepare their meals. Sweepers kept roads, house floors and toilets clean. Dhobi's washed and ironed our clothes.

The school was a few minutes walk away from the teachers' quarters. We were summoned by a gong at 8 a.m. to the assembly that commenced with a hymn and a short prayer, after which we dispersed to our respective classrooms. We continued classes until 1 p.m. without a break, then we closed for lunch and for the day.

Dongargarh Railway Station

Standards 1 and 2 were combined and assigned to one teacher and Standards 3 and 4 were also combined and assigned to another teacher, in a separate room. The Kindergartens were accommodated in the space at the two ends of the assembly room, with a piano serving as a divider.

As I was new to the school, I was assigned to teach KG 1 and the other teacher taught KG 2. The sports and games were conducted by the teachers, with some help from the parents when needed.

A glaring problem, which was largely ignored, was that some of the colony's disadvantaged children were deprived of the privilege of completing their schooling due to poverty.

To be fair, though, there were no other local English schools after Standard 4 in Dongargarh, and the children were packed off to boarding school. The expense was too much for some with large families.

In Dongargarh, I am proud to say that despite the disadvantages, Anglo-Indian men were always busy earning their wages. The railway station was a hive of activity where drivers, guards, station masters, firemen, signallers, loco foremen and workshop technicians went about their business efficiently; also, the permanent way staff went up and down the lines in trolleys inspecting and repairing lines to avoid accidents. Trains and engines were brought in and shunted out, and returned for servicing after a trip.

The biggest attraction in Dongargarh was the Railway Institute: a double-storey building with sweeping views of the surrounding hills. The billiard table, tennis and card tables occupied most of the ground floor, while the reading nook and bar were in the right hand corner, attended by a caretaker. The upstairs comprised a huge ballroom with its two balconies on either side, and a band stage which also housed a grand piano. The band was local. A train driver was the saxophonist and loco technicians were brilliant guitarists and pianists. They played for the impromptu jam sessions free of charge. In fact, they needed very little persuasion to get a dance session going after a whist drive or other occasions. They never thought of collecting fees in those days.

The outside boasted a well-maintained badminton court and the Anglo-Indian community, which was small, met in groups in the evening. Even the local train drivers would be seen walking down the street and it was popularly called the 'Institutional Walk'. To go there was my daily recreation with a new-found boyfriend. It was so wonderful to find a friend to accompany me to dances and whist drives, and help with the handyman jobs around the quarters.

Every year in December, families went to Calcutta on their railway passes for their annual Christmas shopping spree and returned with toys and gifts for their kids. Anglo-Indian ladies permed their hair and bought clothes in the latest fashion. All this helped to make Christmas more exciting, despite the loan which would be paid later on from their salaries. They didn't fail in their religious duties at Christmas either and supported the pastor, who enjoyed their hospitality.

As time went by, six years to be exact, I looked around for a different experience and accepted a job in a college. There were more duties, less privacy and too much supervision. Although the college provided excellent food, accommodation and higher wages, I missed my privacy, culture, leisure and last, but not least, dear old Dongargarh. So I left the teaching job at the college, got married and went where my husband's job took me.

Not long after, another phase of my life ended when, as a mother of five, I too, hitched my wagon to the immigration train in 1970. As my late husband was an employee of the outgoing Caltex India Limited, we too experienced the difficulty of having no English-speaking schools in Mannmad, so it was under the Caltex star that we afforded the funds and opportunity to fly out together as a family of seven to Australia. Due to the nationalisation of all foreign oil companies, my husband was given a decent redundancy package with which we migrated to Perth in 1970, with our 5 children and have not looked back since.

But there are times, even now, when I think of the howling at nights and the sounds of wild panthers prowling in my backyard and I go back in time ... to Dongargarh. Good old Dongargarh.

Guntakal

William Platel

As I go into the twilight of my life, I look back to those wonderful years of wine and roses, of laughter and fun, dances and whist drives, and of the Christmas season in that special town of my youth, the railway bastion of Guntakal, a famous junction in Andhra Pradesh.

Years have gone like water under a bridge... but let's move the clock backward: on the 18th of December 1956 we arrived on Guntakal station, platform No. 4, to take up employment as apprentice firemen on the Railways. We stood there – Claude Vardon and his cousin Oscar, Nelly Pope, Claude's father and my Dad, Clarence George Platel and I – and we contemplated our fate, having nowhere to go and not knowing anyone. A young TXR, Wally Green, came to our rescue. He took us into his home in Tin Lines as it was known then and is still known by this exotic name, and gave us refreshment and comfort.

Guntakal was a bubbling town wholly dependent on the railways, a hub with connecting lines to Hubli, Bangalore, Bombay, Secunderabad, Guntur and Madras. The majority of the worker bees, those in charge of the shed or the drivers or traffic personnel like guards, controllers, TXRs and others, were Anglo-Indians.

Our Community members from other pockets of India had contributed to the Railways, Telegraphs, Customs, Armed Forces, Merchant Navy and Nursing. Guntakal was not going to be left behind. Hundreds of Anglo-Indians from here made a mark for themselves on the Railways.

Gooty is only 18 kms away from Guntakal; it is famous for its historic Tippu Sultan's Fort and the District Taluk's criminal court inside the fort complex. This small station's broad gauge loco shed was another hive of Anglo-Indian activity and was considered an extension to Guntakal's AI family.

In Guntakal we had so many stalwarts as drivers, ones like Lambi Gallyot whom I had the pleasure to work with as his fireman. I learnt so much from legends like him which stood me in good stead in the years to come. Other greats were drivers Noel Godfrey, Jimmy Walsh, Conlon, Vint, Berkley; controllers Ringrow, Baker and not forgetting officers like Rosario, Rapson, Corry, Stan Pougnet, Asst. Security Officer Gomez, the chargemen Moreyra (later loco foreman), Harry Boon, Bastian, boiler chargeman Joe Nicholas affectionately known as Pappa Joe who was a warm, big-hearted person; he ran an open house and mess for the bachelor boys giving them wholesome meals and food prepared by Annie Aunty, lovely tasty dishes made in true AI tradition. Mrs. Soans was another legend in hospitality in Guntakal. So many more whose greatness was a household word and have gone beyond the blue horizon.

The traffic department contributed giants like Lewellyn Butcher, Les Fernandez, Gussy Fernandez, Nicholas, Murray and many more. In the teaching field we had Mrs. Vaughan, Daphne Briggs, Estella Fernandez, Mrs. Pougnet to name a few – they were teachers from good old AI stock. Matron Murray ran a strict and steady hospital with nurses like Mary Nicholas, Mrs. Starr, Bella Briggs and the Boon sisters Esther and Noreen.

The Christmas season was the be all and the end all of everything, a time for romance and laughter, fun and games. The All-India Anglo-Indian Association would run the functions right from 23rd December starting with

A gathering at the Railway Institute – Farewell to Noel & Hazel Godfrey on the eve of their departure from Guntakal, 8th January 1967

Photo courtesy: Roy Baker

the children's tea and sports, then the usual Christmas dance, whist drive, fancy dress and the pound social.

The icing on the cake was the New Year's Ball. All the boys would be on leave for the whole season and go back to work on the 2nd of January. Guntakal was not a very big railway junction, but it afforded us Anglo-Indians the luxury of working, dreaming and marrying our sweethearts and raising good children.

We had graduated from goods drivers to passenger and express trains and were also joined by other Gooty Anglo-Indian boys like Roy Baker, N.J. Hughes, M.T. Popley, Dougie Berger, Phillip Gilles to name a few. Dougie was my old school friend; we both grew up together, studied in St. Joseph's College, Coonoor, Nilgiris, and went on to work as brother drivers, ending our years as drivers of the prestigious Rajdhani Express.

Sports and Inter-Division activities like hockey, volleyball and boxing were held regularly and our Anglo-Indian teams carried our Guntakal colours to Madras and later to Secunderabad when the junction went to the South Central Railway.

Time and tide wait for no man and most of our Guntakal folk have flown, some to Aussie land, some to good old Blighty and some are pushing up the daisies. Memories are made up of things both great and small and it is heartening to see that our present crop of Anglo-Indian youngsters are striving and doing well in the field of Information Technology and also the various commercial sectors. That we are a breed that adapts to present trends and new concepts and can compete with the best of the modern world is very evident.

Trichinopoly Junction and Golden Rock

Harry MacLure

In the late Sixties, when I was a young lad, I remember my Dad taking me on his old Hercules bicycle to the beef and pork stalls which were across the railway lines from where we lived in Trichinopoly, now called Tiruchirapalli or Trichy for short. I also recall in that short 10-minute ride, my Dad would stop to talk to at least five or six Anglo-Indian friends enroute. In those days, when we went out in Trichy, we never failed to bump into fellow Anglo-Indians on the road – the old Junction was literally swarming with our folk; most of them were railway employees. And the lovely thing was, everyone knew everyone else, so much so weddings and funerals were never small affairs.

Being a railwayman's son, and growing up in this not-so-small South Indian railway town, I was fortunate to experience all aspects of Anglo-Indian camaraderie and bonhomie.

My Dad was initially a steam locomotive driver but opted to switch over to driving those handsome diesel rail coaches that were imported from Japan. Trichy was famous for these rail coaches that used to shuttle passengers from Trichy to Mayavaram, Tanjore, Manaparai, Manamadurai, Pudukottai and other small neighbouring towns. The diesel rail cars were quite popular with passengers because they were faster and cleaner than the trains hauled by steam locomotives.

'Jimmy' Richard James MacLure , Driver – Diesel Rail Car (outer signal – Trichinopoly Junction) – 1965.

Taking a ride in the driver's cabin with my Dad was the most thrilling experience of my life. For an 8-year-old boy, it was the ultimate adventure to be seated next to his Dad, cutting across green paddy fields and passing through tiny railway stations and waving at goatherds and village people close to the tracks.

Trichinopoly is an ancient town famous for its 90-metre-archean rock (popularly called Rock Fort) which is to the right of the Cauvery River. The cave temple built by Mahendra Varma, the Pallava King in the sixth century, attracts thousands of devotees and tourists from all parts of the world.

In the eighteenth century, Trichy was the place of repeated conflicts in the battle for supremacy between the British and the French. Historical figures like Robert Clive, Stringer Lawrence, Joseph Francois Dupleix, even Hyder Ali and Tippu Sultan, played prominent roles in the stormy past of this town.

And even to this day, the Trichinopoly cigar or cheroot is well-known by people in the West; these cigars that were hand-made in Trichy were one of India's main items of export during the Victorian era.

As soon as the railway lines from Madras to the deeper South were laid, Trichinopoly started to grow and the Anglo-Indian population grew along with the town.

Trichy is divided into two parts – the Rock Fort and the Cantonment areas. Anglo-Indians mainly lived in the Cantonment and in the Railway Colony that skirts the railway station known simply as 'Junction'. Adjacent to the station's entrance is the building of the Divisional Headquarters of the Southern Railway – an impressive structure that one cannot miss seeing.

Rock Fort – a view from the Cauvery River bridge

The huge 7-platform station, even in those days, was always busy with trains running in or pulling out and passengers either alighting or boarding them. The station provided good retiring rooms and refreshment rooms for weary passengers. No Anglo-Indian visitor coming to Trichy to attend its famous dances would ever want to stay in a hotel; the retiring rooms were perfect for them to rest, shower, dress and walk down along the railway lines to the Institute which is not too far from the station.

The Railway Institute in Trichy was built in 1897 and is still in good shape. As they say, if only the Institute had a tongue, it could tell many an Anglo-Indian tale: the growth of the Community, the love stories, the engagements, the weddings, the anniversaries, the dances, the sporting events, the socials, the bands that became a rage, the Association meetings, the hot gossip, the fisticuffs that no one took seriously, send-off parties thanks to emigration, and the sad decline of the Community...

A main bridge that went over the railway lines, connecting the Toll-gate to the Cantonment, separated the Institute from the now defunct steam loco shed. From atop the bridge, one could always look down at the massive shed and yard and see our men folk sweating it out while on duty. Anglo-Indian railway employees – officers, drivers, firemen, cleaners, guards, ticket collectors, station masters, chargemen, foremen, fitters and even khalasis – were dedicated workers; they simply loved their jobs. It was no wonder that they were held in high esteem by their superiors.

* * *

There were days when a few school pals and I used to walk from Toll-gate, where we lived, to our school in Golden Rock. We did it for the fun of it. Taking a bus, at times, became too boring. The 45-minute walk was never too daunting, especially for us boys with catapults and groundnut sweets in our pockets. The distance from Trichy to Golden Rock is walkable, at least for youngsters like us who felt that everything we did was a big adventure.

The Anglo-Indian Railway High School in Golden Rock was where I did my initial schooling before my family moved to Madras. My three sisters and brother, who are older than me, finished their High School at this institution. It was built in the shape of the alphabet T and was situated on a large portion of railway land in the colony. Most of the teachers and our headmistress were Anglo-Indian. Even though the Railway School was considered inferior by some as compared to the famous Campion and the 250-year-old Vestry in Trichy, I believe it gave its students a good foundation, especially in the English language. The Golden Rock Railway School, I recall, had wonderful and patient Anglo-Indian teachers who taught us well and prepared us to face life outside the colony.

The Golden Rock Railway Station

From my classroom window, I could see the strange gold-brown rock, its 140-feet-high presence dominating the vast railway colony, the nearby railway workshop, and both the

Protestant and Catholic Churches in the colony. A unique feature of the Rock are the five mammoth water reservoirs built on its sides by the British in 1927. The capacity of each tank is 30 lakh litres. Water from the Cauvery River is brought and stored to meet the needs of the railway colonies of Trichy, Golden Rock, and the workshops.

Golden Rock – a view from the Railway Colony

How did this ancient Rock get its name? one may ask. In Tamil the Rock is called Ponmalai, a name believed to be derived from the Poneswari Amman Temple located on it; and in Tamil *pon* means gold and *malai* means hill. Another version says that centuries ago the Rock used to glow or glitter like gold during sunset, hence the name. And yet another – the 'Anglo-Indian version' – (I love this one!) says that Robert Clive, who headed a small force hunting for a troublesome renegade, camped at the Rock. When they left the vantage point, Clive hid some of his plundered gold in a secret cave in the Rock (with an intention of coming back for it, but for some reason never did.) "The gold is still there! You want to be a rich man? Just search the Rock!" I've heard this from many an Anglo-Indian old timer in Golden Rock. And like so many youngsters in those simpler times, I too harboured the thought of becoming rich overnight by finding Clive's gold!

Very close to the Rock and on the fringes of the colony, a residential locality grew on private land. Ponmalaipatti became a hub for retired Anglo-Indian railway employees who bought land and built small bungalows. This locality is well known for its famous Franklyn Club; Anglo-Indian meetings and get-togethers even to this day are conducted at this club.

The Golden Rock railway station, a mere two miles away from Trichy Junction, was and still is a favoured stop for colony residents and for people living in Ponmalaipatti. In those days, *jhutkas* used to be parked by the station's entrance; today one would see only autorickshaws.

The station is not too far from the Golden Rock Railway Institute and the railway workshop. In 1897, the South Indian Railways set up its central workshops at Nagapatinam (near Vailankanni Church), principally to repair and maintain steam locomotives. But because of its strategic location, Trichy was later chosen, and the workshops were moved in 1928 to its present site in Golden Rock where it continues to function on a total area of 200 acres.

The workshop had started off with modern facilities rarely seen in those early years. A massive power-station generated electricity for the workshop as well as the colony, which was one of the first places in Trichy to be lit by electrical lights.

During the Second World War, the Golden Rock workshop housed an Armoury that stored weapons and ammunition; the workshop was also involved in the repairing of Royal Air Force's air planes.

Over 6,000 employees of varied ranks worked at the shops and more than half of them were Anglo-Indians. So one could safely assume that in the forties, fifties and even sixties, there were over 10,000 Anglo-Indians working and living in Golden Rock.

For those Anglo-Indians who grew up in Golden Rock, Christmas time in the colony must have been really grand; every other house in the colony would have belonged to an Anglo-Indian family spreading the Season's joy and Christian spirit. They had their own dances at their Institute. Trichy folk attended the Golden Rock shows and the Golden Rock crowd reciprocated by supporting theirs, but there was always an undercurrent of friendly rivalry between the two groups.

* * *

Trichy and Golden Rock still have a sizeable Anglo-Indian population as compared to other smaller railway towns in India; but unlike in the past, there are only a handful of our folk who work on the railways today. On a recent trip to Trichy – to visit one of my sisters who lives there with her family – I was a little disappointed that I did not bump into fellow Anglo-Indians on the road. A motorbike ride to Golden Rock took me to the railway station, the Institute and finally to my old school. All the landmarks, including the railway colony and the railway parks, once lovely, now wear a forlorn look. As for the Rock... its golden glow seems to have gone... only Heaven knows where!

A Town called Jolarpet

Royston Edwards

Jolarpet is a Railway Junction on the Madras-Bangalore and Madras-Erode lines about 140 miles from Madras. I think the station did have a Higginbothams book store and Spencer outlet. I definitely remember the first class waiting room. The waiting room was usually utilised by Anglo-Indians and some Indian Officers and their families. The room was well furnished with padded chairs and western toilets, which were clean and well maintained.

The station was always busy, even at night, due to the heavy train traffic in both directions. Jolarpet (JTJ as it was called in railway parlance) was a banking station and depot for all trains bound from Erode, Arkonam and Bangalore. Engines were filled with coal and water and the locomotive crew would be changed. I used to marvel at the skill of the AI drivers who maneuvered their engines so skillfully to stop exactly below the re-fuelling point. Besides their skills they also had limited time to accomplish the re-fuelling procedure. I can picture the Brindavan Express steaming through JTJ with a WP engine and its tender and carriages painted green, to take on water at three stops, Katpadi, JTJ and Bangarapet. Trains to Banglore had to be banked due to the ghat section.

East and West of the station were the quarters for the traffic branch, guards and station masters, yardmasters. North of the station were the quarters for the running staff, officers and teachers. Depending on the classification of individual employees, appropriate living quarters were allocated.

JTJ had a very big Railway Institute for Anglo-Indians, a Railway School, Catholic and Protestant Churches. I still remember the Institute dance floor as a little boy, sliding, gliding and spreading the French chalk while the elders jived, fox-trotted and waltzed to the music of Kolar Gold Fields' bands.

My Grandpa Joe Edwards, who had retired at the time, practically lived at the Institute playing skittles and billiards. The Institute had two full sized billiards tables. I remember the marker doing the scoring for the players. Christmas season was great fun with functions galore at the Institute. New Year's eve bonfire was another bright light for my 8-year-old mind, especially the Good Fairy chasing the old man around the fire!

The beauty of JTJ was the Yelagiri Hills, which formed a back-drop to the place. Sunrise was a sight to behold, with the sun rising slowly above the crest. It was a similar experience to watch the moon rising on clear nights.

I cannot forget the butcher stalls as the Anglo-Indians loved eating bull. Our favourites were liver, tongue, brain, cowheel, trotters and kutty pie... Mutton was expensive and only the high-salary earners could afford it. Servants did the daily morning shopping with their cane baskets.

We used to buy tomatoes, green chillies, pieces of coconut, drumsticks, snake gourd and brinjals from the local market. English vegetables and butter were bought in Russell Market, Bangalore, by only those who could afford it. Most AI homes had a meat-safe and dinner-wagons, in which they displayed their good crockery. The legs of the meat-safe had to be

Circa 1950 – Fr. Ladislaus with Anglo-Indian ladies of Jolarpet who belonged to the Legion of Mary Group; some of the members seen in this photograph are Mrs. Dashwood (Jolarpet), Mrs. Jeremiah (Arkonam), Mrs. Armstead (Melbourne) and Mrs. Pinch (Melbourne)

Photo courtesy: Royston Edwards

inserted in containers, usually old jam tins with water, to prevent ants from getting to the eatables stored within.

Jolarpet had a few streets which were lined with huge neem, banyan and tamarind trees. These trees were filled with lots of birds, squirrels and monkeys. All grown-ups were called "Aunty" or "Uncle" and if any of us got caught doing something wrong, we heard this phrase: "Wait till I tell your mother or father, you will get your back-side tanned," or "slipper-whacked!"

Most households reared fowls, ducks and pigeons. The favourite sports for some railwaymen were gamecock and quail fights. Fowl curry, duck, quail or pigeon roast were popular items on our menu.

The Gurkhas were employed by the VIPs to patrol the Railway Colony at night. They would strike their sticks on the door steps and blow their whistles to make known their presence. Then there was the Call-Boy who would knock on the bedroom window calling "Saar! Saar!" in the ungodly hours of the night.

When I was 11 years old I was packed off to the boarding school at Campion in Trichy. Most AIs went to St. Bede's, St. Patrick's or St. George's in Madras. Girls went to St. Francis Xavier's fondly called the "Bun & Plantain" school or Holy Angels. There were lots of Guntakal, Hubli and Bangalore boys who went to Campion as well. So I had company as they all had to pass JTJ.

Those journeys to and from school were great fun. I would like to mention some of my fun days at JTJ. We were neighbours to a family called Robsons who had five sons, three of them older than me. These boys were full of tricks as they carried "katties" (catapults) in one pocket and stones, pori cudlay, kirks, coconut and jaggery in the other. These boys were crack shots with the katty, their favourite targets being buffies or blood suckers (tree lizards). Sometimes they even shot a squirrel, a bird or tickled up the monkeys perched on top of a mango tree. They even had a competition to shoot the bulb (globe) on top of a lamp post. But they made sure that the bulbs they shot were not the ones nearest to their houses.

The Robson boys were experts at making katties and they specially selected the katty sticks from guava trees. They checked the size and grip on the tree before they cut it off. Vacuum rubbers from the locomotives were excellently split in half with a 7 O'Clock razor blade to a specific tension and strength. A soft piece of leather obtained from the chuckler under the tamarind tree was carefully cut to size to make the pouch. The katty was christened when they shot the first buffy with its blood smeared on the katty stick.

Another aspect of the Colony that comes to mind is the railway loco shed siren. The siren was sounded at 7 a.m., 11 a.m., 12 noon, 1 p.m. and 5 p.m., which were the timings for loco maintenance staff. At times it went off in the night repeatedly and this was the signal for the emergency staff to show up for duty as a result of an accident or derailment. The railway quarters got water supplied for their use once in the morning and once in the evening.

Like so many other AIs in those days, my parents decided to leave India and in 1973 we emigrated to Melbourne, Australia. In 1976 I met and married my lovely wife Carolyn, who also left JTJ when she was 13 years old. When Carolyn cooked our first meal she did not know the difference between turmeric and chilli powder. Today she is my masala dosai and Mysore pak queen.

Carolyn used to enjoy eating jumlums, star gooseberries and Indian sweets sold by the ding-ding man, who came around the Colony at night. Since both of us were from the same town, we are always able to reminisce about those good old days...

Jamalpur Revisited

Darryl Burke

It is just thirty short hours since I left Jamalpur. I step down from the crowded compartment of the Upper India Express and make my way to the station exit. It had been around 8 p.m. on the 8th of August. We of the '71 batch had waved goodbye to our juniors as our train pulled slowly out of Jamalpur. We had been on our way to Asansol for further training. Most of us had not known if we would see Jamalpur again. But now, as early as 2 a.m. on the 10th, I have come back, heartily bluffing myself that I have tons of unfinished business to attend to; once inside the station, however, I realise that I have come only to revisit my professional birthplace, I experience a feeling which many others who have left Jamalpur on completion of workshop training, and have made the mistake of coming back too soon, must have experienced.

Yes, coming back to Jamalpur so soon has been a mistake, I reflect, as I cross the low bridge and walk down the only two Jamalpur roads to the Hostel which was home to me for more than three and a half years. 'Nothing has changed, of course, in the short time that I have been away. Only I have aged. Jamalpur is somehow no longer mine, except to roam at will; as I pass the Indian Railways Institute of Mechanical and Electrical Engineering, I remember the four School Sessions

I completed here with a sense of detachment that was nowhere in evidence just two days ago.

The famous workshop – 1897:
Jamalpur was the first of the major railway towns, built and administered by the railways and populated entirely by railway employees.

The feeling of not belonging grows I walk up to the Hostel and climb over the gate I have climbed over dozens of times before. I hesitate outside the door of my room. Rather, the room which had been mine – then, realising that I have no option, I enter, I make my way unerringly in the dark to my locker, switch on the light, and open it. The few articles remaining, further depress me by acting as a reminder of the many things my locker had been stuffed with, fill me with a sense of regret. They, at least, are mine; I shall be taking them with me. But Jamalpur, as a whole, is now for me an empty shell filled with memories that have gone stale overnight.

I wake up at about 6.30 a.m. and spend the day busying myself with the unfinished business that had given me an excuse to revisit Jamalpur. As I move around, I see every road, every tree, every building as if for the first time – and the last. It is a unique experience, that thrills while it saddens. My mind goes back to the 16th of January 1971, the day I first set eyes on Jamalpur. A week earlier the letter calling me to join the Railway as an apprentice had reached me at my house in Calcutta.

The morning was cold as I stepped down on the platform. Although it was past 10 in the morning, my breath condensed into small puffs of moisture. I booked my luggage in the parcels office and, after asking directions of the Ticket Collector, took a rickshaw to the Workshop gate. The rest of that day is a blur of memories now, memories of rushing from office to office, memories of a missing certificate and a lost bond form, of an early lunch and a late tea in the dining hall where I was to have my meals for the next three and a half years.

The years passed as time passes in a hostel. For the first time in my life, I played cricket, football and hockey. Always a late riser, I learned the joy of getting up before dawn and going for a morning walk or run before the sun rose to warm the day. I experienced a year of floods culminating in an exceptionally severe winter, followed by a really blistering summer. Never having travelled much, I reveled in the three Technical Tours which took me to all corners of the country. The School Sessions were a challenge, as were the Workshop Interviews. Here in Jamalpur I learned how to wind an armature, read printers' proofs, operate a telephone board and run a mess. I suffered from jaundice, influenza, and also plain and simple hypochondria. And I came to know the sorrow of departure, the momentary exhilaration of being 'tossed' in the traditional style on the railway platform, the rush of shaking what seemed to be a thousand hands, of forgiving and being forgiven old faults, of being garlanded and gifted. The farewell was, to me, a funeral. Even as the train pulled out of the station, I knew that the Jamalpurean in me was slowly dying and I mourned his passing with farewell tears. I should have known better than to come searching for his spirit.

Darryl Burke then and now

Early tomorrow morning I shall go to the hills for a last walk around. Already I know it will not be worth the effort. The hills of Jamalpur are just one more of the many things I am dead to, like the Technical School and the Hostel. Nevertheless I shall go, and from the top of the hill, take one last look across the town to the green fields and, beyond, the river Ganges. I know I shall not be able to recapture the carefreeness of an early morning stroll as I had known it before I bid Jamalpur farewell. The ties have been severed, and I shall never be able to splice them. I shall always cherish memories of my life here. But, to my eternal sorrow, Jamalpur is no longer home to me... no, not even if I revisit it a thousand times.

Editor's Note:

LAST MAN OUTSTANDING

This picture taken from The Anglo-Indian Review of Nov.-Dec. 1975 shows Darryl Burke receiving the prestigious Silver Medal for studies, the highest award for his category, from the then General Manager, Eastern Railway, Mr. Sawhney. He is also the first Anglo-Indian to win this top award.

Darryl is undoubtedly the last of a long line of Anglo-Indian Apprentice Mechanics (Engineers) trained in Jamalpur Workshop by the Indian Railways Institute of Mechanical and Electrical Engineering.

Darryl, the son of Albert and Evelyn Burke of Calcutta, joined the Eastern Railway as an Apprentice Mechanic (Electrical) at Jamalpur Workshop in 1971.

He left Railway service in 1982 to join the ONGC (Oil and Natural Gas Commission). He retired as Chief Engineer (Electrical) ONGC and is now settled at Margao, Goa.

Khurda . . . as it was!

Noel Thomas

In the Nineteen Forties – even up to the early Fifties – people would ask you: "Khurda Road, where on earth is that?"

Khurda Road (KUR in railway parlance) was not even on the Indian postal map. Its post office was and is still called 'Jatni'. KUR was just a railway station of the erstwhile Bengal Nagpur Railway (BNR), in the Puri district of Orissa.

The Calcutta and Madras-bound Mails crossed at KUR, just after midnight. The G.S. or W.P. steam locomotive would detach from the train for 'loco requirements', over the ash pit, under the water column. The loco might even be changed. Yet, except for the pleasant little bump as the driver re-attached, passengers bound for Calcutta, Madras or in-between, felt nothing. They slept on, blissfully unaware of KUR's existence.

At such an ungodly hour, there wasn't the usual cacophony of railway stations, no sing-song of Chai! Kaafee! Instead, there was an eerie silence as a few passengers embarked or disembarked unobtrusively.

All this gave KUR a certain label of obscurity, of insignificance – residents of larger railway colonies were inclined to dismiss it as a small, quiet place. Well, small it certainly was, compared to Kharagpur, Waltair, Bilaspur or Nagpur, in terms of area and civic amenities, but insignificant – certainly not! Square mile for square mile, person for person, KUR was one of the liveliest railway colonies on the BNR and one of the friendliest as well.

Tourists bound for the famous Jaganath and Konark temples at Puri, twenty-seven miles away, had to change trains at KUR junction during the day. They would vouch for the friendliness of KUR's railway staff and certify the 'poori-tac' as the tastiest along the line.

The station building was far from imposing, but the restaurant was well-stocked and well-managed. Mr. Sequeira was an excellent cook who turned out very tasty food, unlike the bland, insipid stuff one usually got in railway caterings those days.

The railway staff, guards, station masters, ticket collectors, were immaculately dressed, shining, resplendent in their uniforms.

From the top of the foot over bridge, one could see the steam Loco Shed with the black beauties: G.C.Ses, G.Ses, H.Ses, HSMs, WGs and WPs gleaming in the sun. KUR was a passenger shed, at one time housing 40 locomotives. The Loco Foreman was in charge of the shed. Foremen of calibre such as Slaney, Sargent, Bertie Stuart and Paul with efficient maintenance teams led by experienced Head Fitters and Boiler Makers such as Jossy Lovery, Leslie Hendricks, Pat D'Brass, Ginger Shreeves, Sammy Hale and others, kept the engines in good fettle. Drivers like Kenny Naylor, Alec Betreen, Ben McCoy and Sammy Barren were married to their engines – they spent more time with them than with their wives. While the drivers romanced their 'Iron Horses', their wives became familiar with intimate parts like the regulator, lever, lubricator and injector. The wives of running staff were of course 'iron ladies' in their own right – they had to be, with their menfolk 'on line' most of the time. Youngsters had another interest in the shed apart from the engines. They went there to collect old piston rings to use as 'bandies', and discarded vacuum cylinder rubber rolling rings for their catapults.

In the railway market, a morning shopper would notice Bazaar Master, Willie Cooper, inspecting the items on display and putting his 'A1' stamp of approval on cuts of mutton in the butcher stall.

'J.B. Thackers' was the only big departmental store. This shop stood out among the small, nondescript ration and vegetable shops. JB's brother, D.P. Thacker, sold his wares in the colony, carrying them in boxes and bundles – cloth, ribbons, lace, etc.. He was well known as 'Walking Thacker'. 'Cheap Jack' (never got to know his real name) was another house-to-house pedlar of knick-knacks and cheap consumables.

The railway colony consisted of bungalows, monkey blocks and kholies (servant quarters) or out-houses. Running staff, guards and drivers were housed close to the station in bungalow-type quarters. Foremen and Inspectors had larger bungalows.

A Small Monkey Block

Photo courtesy: Arline D'Souza

Kholies were allotted to residents of bungalows/monkey blocks, according to designation. Higher ups, officers and senior subordinates would have three or four kholies for their servants, other staff getting two or at least one for their servants.

The provision of kholies was really a blessing, since in those days the average railway household needed three to four servants, a full time ayah, a cook, full time or part time. For powdering and grinding spices, pounding rice, etc., a 'masalachi' was required, so was a mali to fetch water and tend the garden and a mehtar/mehtrani to sweep, swab and clean the chamber pots.

By modern standards, these servants were low-paid, about ten rupees per month, but were happy with the kholi. They were very loyal, virtually household members, especially the ayah who was indispensable. The servants' children mingled and played with the 'babas' and 'missybabas', picking up a lot of English in the process.

The kholies acquired a reputation of their own. Some were even famous like the one in which 'Opper Lakshmi' made and sold delicious 'Hoppers'. We queued up for them, ate them with coconut milk and sugar, or with leftovers – my mouth waters as I write. The notorious kholies were those in which persons like Acchayya and his ilk brewed liquor from rice, wheat, banana and god knows what else, but were patronised by some colony folk who preferred this cheap fire water (country) to the costlier and scarcely available foreign liquor.

The monkey blocks were different. They were older versions of railway apartments with full length jaffrey shutters in front and a spiral staircase at the rear for the servants, particularly for the mehtar/mehtrani to do their rather obnoxious job.

Every railway bungalow had a large compound. Between rows of bungalows, there were wide open spaces, maidans where children and young teenagers played rounders, football and cricket, mostly after school in the evenings, till dusk. One had to be home before the street oil-lamps were lit – to join in the family prayers.

Older teenagers and eligible young men would congregate at strategic spots later in the evening by a cemented culvert underneath the lamp post, for a sing-song to the accompaniment of a Spanish guitar, maybe a mouth-organ too; they would sing their hearts out, hoping the girl they were trying for was within earshot. Sometimes in good humour, a song was directed at a group of girls passing by. These were KUR's lamplight serenades, but it was all good, clean fun and frolic. There was even friendly rivalry with more than one trying for the same girl, but the better man wins was the rule of the game.

This sporting spirit was nurtured on the maidans, with keenly contested 'manly' sports – a fair amount of boxing, too. After the verdict, both the victor and vanquished shook hands and all was forgotten. There was no shame in losing.

There were, of course, some sad but funny incidents, as when Graydon Clarke and Mickey Rozario, seven-year olds, stepped into the ring for the first time and Graydon landed a classic straight left. Mickey burst out crying: "He hit me in the eye!" To him, at the receiving end, this was not quite 'Marquis of Queensbury'. Both these pugilists are now settled in the UK.

Among the famous KUR sportsmen were boxers Malcolm Stuart, Rudolph Keswick, Podgy and Neville Dennis, the famous fraternal football trio of Ronnie, Eardley and Fido Thomas. Ronnie, alas, is no more, Eardley is in Melbourne, Fido is in Perth. There was Norman Parker, the hockey wizard and the brothers Gilbert and Horace Wheeler, who made it to the big Calcutta League. There were many sporting girls – one I remember is Olive Gaudoin (née Rozario), now in the UK, who was a promising junior National athlete.

The same spirit of clean and fair enjoyment was carried over to the Railway Institute. KUR dances seldom ended in a fracas. These shows were expertly managed, ball room etiquette was strictly observed – the MC saw to that. Officers and khalasis were treated alike. As the dancers warmed up, complexes were forgotten, inhibitions were shed, everyone was on the floor, having a good time. If the MC smelt a fight coming on, he would discreetly usher the combatants downstairs, where they settled their differences. The band played a little louder and as Byron put it, "the dance went on and joy was unconfined!"

Ladies Badminton Club, Khurda Road – 1950s. L to R: Pamela Power, Mrs. Power, Anne Lovery, Eleanor Power, Iona James, Winnie Betreen, Sybil Tapsell (Sister of Carl Tapsell) and Dorothy Doll

Photo courtesy: Vivian Lovery (UK)

Many outstation folks came for the KUR dances, mainly from Cuttack and Berhampur. Some of the local big-wigs also came. One might see the D.O.S., the D.C.S., even the S.D.O. of Khurda Town – their posh clubs could not provide such pure entertainment!

Waltair and Kharagpur dance bands were reputed in those days – they played at KUR on occasions. They did have some good musicians, but the KUR crowd loved its own home band, the C.D.A. band (Catholic Debating Academy) with Lionel Martin on the piano, Colin Lovery on the sax and crooning as well, KUR's Bing Crosby, his brother Stanley on the drums, Arthur Nipps on the trumpet, and Winno Hoffland on the double-bass.

The younger generation maintained the tradition. The KUR bandstand once had a famous surprise visitor in Garney Nyss, leader of the 'Aloha Boys' group. Garney was quite taken up with KUR's budding guitarist Bobby Norris. KUR was home to some famous musicians, now abroad; to name a few: Michael DeDombal (Mike Danton), Glaxon Saunders and Neville Antioch of Ontario, Melbourne and Perth respectively.

Every year from 22nd December to the 4th of January, Khurda went into the season with festive abandon – young and old let themselves go – the Christmas programme featured childrens' sports, adults' sports with Pagal Gymkhana, fancy dress for children, whist drives, housie, crown and anchor, married vs. bachelors matches, any number of hops and jam sessions and of course the 26th December Christmas Dance and the 31st New Year Ball. The dancers were well catered for – delicious snacks and coffee were served at separate sittings.

The 31st of course was the Grand Finale – a gala affair. The revelers trooped out of the hall arms linked, caps on, bugles blaring away, part of the Grand March from the Hall to the bonfire on the football field. The band accompanied them. Auld Lang Syne was sung raucously, the natural falsettos for once making themselves heard, but this was an occasion when social harmony was more appreciated than musical harmony. At the stroke of midnight, all the steam locomotives in the shed and the yard whistled together loud and long. It was the sweetest sound you ever heard and time for the wishing to start. Everyone wished everyone.

CDA Band, Khurda Road, 1945.
Back Row: Donald Fernandez and Terence Martin.
Next row: Maggie Fernandez, Colin Lovery, Winoo Hofland, – , Arthur Nipps.
Front Row: Derek Bastian, – , Stanley Lovery

Photo courtesy: Vivian Lovery (UK)

Yet, one must not forget that fun loving though he was, the call of duty was sacred to the Anglo-Indian railwayman. When the accident hooter sounded during the dance, the Accident Relief Train personnel, Loco Foreman, Head Fitter or just plain workman, immediately excused himself from his pretty partner, dashed home and reported in record time in his overalls, to the Relief Train in charge. Duty came first!

A parallel entertainment centre was the Parochial Hall of the Sacred Heart Catholic Church, where there were regular whist drives and occasional dances, but not without certain restrictions.

The Railway Institute was more active with a monthly children's evening, an amateur hour, whist drive, jam sessions and marriage receptions. The children's Christmas tree was also a unique event. Santa came, not on a sleigh, but on a huge pachyderm – courtesy the Raja of Puri, ex-officio Head of the Jaganath Temple – it was the temple elephant, especially chosen to carry the most famous Christmas celebrity! After Santa distributed the toys and emptied his bag of goodies, it was the children's turn to ride the jumbo – quite an enjoyable experience, more thrilling than the merry-go-round ride.

The KUR railway school, though only up to the primary level, was another island of excellence. The headmistress was Sybil Tapsell, a stately dignified lady, sister of the famous hockey Olympians, Carl and Leslie, the former a formidable fullback and short corner specialist. Her brothers had left for Australia earlier.

The school had excellent teachers, Louise Shea, Violet Murray, Maggie Edwards and others, and maintained a good standard. Algebra was taught in Class III ! The BNR conducted a Board Exam for all Primary Schools at Class IV. The annual school concert was a big event. Teachers were devoted and very fair – no extra marks for children with high connections. Merit was the prime consideration. Of course, there was a 'colonial' slant, but the transition from 'God save the King' to 'Jana Gana Mana' and 'Jai Hind' was smooth, spontaneous and without jingoistic overtones.

Most of the Anglo-Indians were Catholics. The Sacred Heart Church was packed on Sunday and feast days. It was heavenly to hear Daisy Hurley's booming soprano voice, Eric Jones' bass one, Tottie Adie on the organ and Cliffy Ambrose on the violin. There were regular Sunday school classes for children. First Communions were grand events. Father Arbizu was a popular parish priest.

The Church of St. John in the Wilderness, the Anglican church, was also well attended. The Pentecostals came later. Sister Mackertich (Sr. Mack) started the Mission School, which has grown into a premier educational institution.

The Railway Hospital took good care of the railwaymen and their wards. Family doctors were available. All babies were home-delivered, either by the railway midwife or the very experienced private midwife, Mrs. Hupping. Dr. Stanley Ambrose was one of the better known private doctors.

There was Joe Trindade, the incomparable prankster who set you off on a wild goose chase or played a practical joke on you, much to your embarrassment, but you could only laugh with him and admire his ingenuity. Joe who is touching ninety, lives in Melbourne now and is still full of mischievous ideas.

KUR had a separate residential colony for its senior citizens – retired railway employees. The institute offered them subsidised membership. They kept themselves occupied with social work at the St. Vincent dePaul Society.

Some ex-KUR folk from across the seas, do come back sometimes, see KUR as it is and some come to see it again. There are others who say, "I've seen it in better days. I don't want to see it now."

Khurda Road Railway Station

Photo courtesy: Arline D'Souza

Khurda Road has survivors – some animate, old familiar faces, some inanimate: the Railway Institute, the Churches, the bungalows, monkey blocks, trees, culverts, 'seats of my youth' as Goldsmith says. They still beckon to me, these silent sentinels of the past and each time I'm near them, happy memories begin to flood my consciousness. I look back with pleasure and pride, then turn around again and march on with hope and confidence.

Memories of Kharagpur

Shane Calvert

"Any connection with the long past – a reference to forgotten events and personages, and to manners, feelings, and opinions, almost or wholly obsolete – will serve to illustrate how much of old material goes to make up the freshest novelty of human life."

– *Nathaniel Hawthorne*

My hometown, Kharagpur, will always remain an integral part of my life. The childhood memories will always remain deeply embedded in the recesses of my mind. My earliest recollections of school are the four years I spent in the South Eastern Railway English Medium High School, known as the European High School long before my time. My first teacher, Mrs. Mary Hurst, an Anglo-Indian, never fails to fondly remind me, whenever we meet, how little I was then. My next teacher was Mrs. Tina Francis followed by Mrs. Daphne Clarke, both Anglo-Indians. I distinctly remember, Mrs. Scolt, our music teacher, who introduced us to the richness of melodies and the myriad rhythms of life. All that became a distant past when I was shifted to La Martiniere For Boys, Calcutta, the school immensely responsible for moulding and shaping my life and character.

Kharagpur, about 110 kms away from Kolkata, is remembered as home in Anglo-Indian memory and finds a mention in histories and fiction dealing with the Anglo-Indian community. A vibrant Anglo-Indian community existed in Kharagpur until the early 1960s when the exodus began. Very little remains of that remembered past, yet the image of Kharagpur as recalled by senior residents is that of an idyllic colonial outpost with a quintessential Raj lifestyle.

Kharagpur Railway Station

Owen Clement, an Anglo-Indian writer from Kharagpur, reminisces about his hometown in his book 'Highlights in the Shadows', in the following words:

"....The original village of Kharagpur, situated on a red sandy plain seventy-two miles (110 kilometres) south west of Calcutta in West Bengal, was rebuilt as a railway junction in the year 1900. Civil engineer Colonel C. W. Bowles was appointed by the Bengal Nagpur Railway Company to take charge of constructing its workshops, houses, schools, churches, hospitals, armoury, recreational facilities and a gaol, which once boasted of two very important political prisoners, Subhas Chandra Bose and Jawaharlal Nehru."

The residential area was built on the European plan of broad streets and open spaces. Six avenues ran East-West parallel to the main rail lines. The residents along First and Second avenues were the lower subordinate staff. The more senior locomotive drivers, workshop chargemen and foremen were housed along Third and Fourth avenues. The palatial officers homes and grounds were situated along Fifth and Sixth avenues.

The native Gole Bazaar where the residents did their grocery shopping, was spread out on the other side of the tracks.

The golf course was nothing more than an open area called the Chandmari Maidan on the town's southern outskirts, set aside for the town's future development.

Some hockey historians say that Kharagpur was the Mecca of Indian Hockey, producing star players who represented BNR in the Beighton Cup. Brothers Carl and Les Tapsell, Dicky Carr, Joe Gallibardy and Leslie Claudius are the immortals of our hockey glory.

Tapsell, Carr and Gallibardy, the brilliant BNR trio, represented India at the Berlin Olympics in 1936. While Carr dazzled with his stickwork, Gallibardy and Tapsell were penalty corner pioneers - Gallibardy invented the short corner to push the ball and Carl Tapsell was the lethal conversion specialist.

Dicky Carr was also part of the 4 x 100 metres relay team at the 1932 Olympics along with Ronald Vernieux and Bunoo Sutton.

Leslie Claudius, four-time Olympic medalist and one of the biggest names in Indian Hockey, also started his hockey career in Kharagpur.

Gerry Glacken a 1948 Olympian is believed to have been from Kharagpur.

Jenny Boland (Sanderson), who played at Wimbledon as a sixteen year old, was also from Kharagpur.

There were other sporting families – the Hills, Lennons, Roches, Watsons, Wainwrights, Bunyans, Halls, boxers Arthur Brown and Vivian D'Cruze, billiard wizards Trevor Gaudoin and Peter Edwards.

Anglo-Indian ladies, Mrs. Peacock, Mrs. Henderson, Mrs. Paul, Mrs. Gaudoin, Mrs. Shreeves, were dedicated nurses in the Railway Hospital.

Every young boy of my generation has dreamt of being an engine driver. I remember with pleasure the trips to the loco shed, to find out trip details of my father Ronnie. There were occasions when he took me and my two younger brothers, Troy and Tyronne to the loco shed (my sister Sabrina, the youngest, never got this opportunity) and it was quite an experience to get on the footplate holding on to the stanchion rod. It was considered manly to shovel coal from the chute into the fire box.

My father Ronnie retired as a loco inspector. How he joined the railways is a fascinating story. It was the summer of 1956 and the schools were on vacation. The young Anglo-Indian boys and girls were out playing a game of 'rounders' on Beighton grounds when a huge van came along. Mr. Green, the then DME, hopped out.

Seeing the tall strapping gentleman in uniform, accompanied by police personnel walking up to them, frightened the youngsters. He called the boys, (seventeen of them) and asked them if they wanted to work and earn some money. At that time there was an All India railway strike on and the Anglo-Indians were known to stay away from such disruptions in the railways because work for them was a matter of pride, and loyalty and dedication was intrinsic to their nature. All seventeen very excitedly agreed and were asked to hop onto the van which took them directly to the loco shed where they were assigned to assist Anglo-Indian drivers and shunters and to keep the wheels moving. Tying a handkerchief on the forehead and holding a shovel in the hand was the ultimate achievement for an Anglo-Indian lad. That was the end of school and the beginning of a journey on the railways. From a second fireman to fireman, shunter, mail driver and then as a loco inspector, the journey was a highly satisfying one.

We were fed on stories of Anglo-Indian railwaymen, stories that were told with a great deal of pride and a sense of accomplishment.

Waiting for the signal: 1960s
(L to R): Ronnie Calvert, Derek Callaghan and Leslie Thomas in the cab.

Photo courtesy: Shane and Ronnie Calvert (KGP)

Daryl Kitchen was hit by an electric lamp post while working the Bombay Mail from Howrah to CKP. Despite the serious head injury he brought his train to its destination, stepped out of the engine, collapsed on the platform and was declared dead on arrival.

Driver Crizzle, while working the Janata Express 38 down, was given a wrong signal and to his utter surprise found that a goods train 313 was on the same track. He dropped vacuum, slowed the train down, lessened the impact and saved the lives of the passengers but lost his own.

The Railway Institute was the centre of all social activities, where whist drives, housie (bingo) nights, dances, costume parties, tin-and-bottle badminton tournaments and sports events were organized.

From the Children's Christmas Tree to the New Year Ball, Christmas was an event which was looked forward to with a great deal of excitement by the Anglo-Indians.

A trip to Calcutta was always on the cards in the run up to the festive period. Toys for the children, dried fruits and nuts, barley sugar, 'bandel cheese', marzipans, ham, bacon and sausages had to be on the list of items to be bought besides many other things.

Christmas cake-making was another enjoyable ritual.

There were specialties like salt-meat. I must confess that I have quite mastered the art of preparing it, passed on to me by my mother Audrey, who served as a teacher at Sacred Heart School. I hope to pass on this skill to my two sons, Wade and Arran. My wife Andrea, who is also a trained teacher, does an excellent job of preparing ginger wine.

By the time I reached my late teens perceptible changes had taken place. The main hall of the Institute had been converted to a permanent cinema hall and the billiard room and bar on the first floor was shut. That marked the end of the legendary dances and the lovely wooden floor, on which many a lasting romance was forged, was ripped apart to make way for a cold, cemented, sloping floor. The bandstand, which for years stood in resplendent glory, was reduced to ruins – a sad end to a relic of a rich past. The only old-age charm that remained was the hair dressing saloon at the other end of the Institute, with its typical western setting, with swing doors and long mirrors framed in solid teak.

Kharagpur Railway Institute & Bandstand, 1930s

Community-based activities then shifted to the Parochial hall, the community centre of Sacred Heart Church. Summer camps and dances were then held there. By then music trends had undergone a sea change, but dances had to have the all-time favourites – jive, waltz and foxtrot. An Anglo-Indian just knew how to shake a leg.

While many believe that the Community is fast disappearing, I am of the opinion that the Anglo-Indian has reinvented himself/herself to face the new challenges that India has thrown at us. Anglo-Indians have rapidly assimilated into the culture and tradition of our country, and have yet held on to their own unique identity and traditions.

Behind the statement 'I am an Anglo-Indian' is a rich slice of history, both political and personal. We are what someone said, "an exotic cocktail", that has "matured and become a unique aromatic spirit, generously flavoured and very stimulating".

The Heroism of Mack Johannes

Shane Calvert

On the 5th of January 2013, when ex-Martinians met at Calcutta's Tollygunge Club for a reunion, Mr. Chakravarthy, Principal of La Martiniere for Boys, came up to me and asked me to meet a Michael Johannes, who had an interesting story to tell.

Michael's father, Mack Johannes, was a driver in the South Eastern Railway at Kharagpur.

On the night of 26th July 1956, while Johannes was driving the 315 UP passenger train from Jokpur towards Kharagpur, just before midnight, there was a sudden blow-back of fiery gases from the fire-box door where he was standing with his two firemen.

Caught in the flames, all three men were seriously injured The two firemen decided to save their lives and jumped off the moving train. Trapped in the enveloping flames and facing certain death unless he followed the firemen, Johannes decided to sacrifice his life in order to save the lives of the passengers (about four hundred) on his train. Inspired by this high resolve, though in terrible pain and badly burnt in the inferno, he succeeded in halting the train near the outer signal of Kharagpur station. Then, with exemplary courage, he staggered painfully back to the rear of the train and informed the guard of what had occurred. Johannes was rushed to the hospital where he succumbed to his injuries within a few hours. He is survived by his widow Marjorie and son Michael who emigrated to Sydney in 1966.

For his devotion to duty, heroic action and self-sacrifice, Mack Johannes was posthumously awarded the Ashoka Chakra.

Dr. Rajendra Prasad, President of India, talking to Mrs. Marjorie Johannes in connection with the Investiture Ceremony in New Delhi on 11th October 1957. Mr. Mack Johannes, Driver South Eastern Railway, was awarded the Ashoka Chakra Class II posthumously for his heroic action and self-sacrifice.

Photo courtesy: Shane Calvert

Michael went on to narrate how years later, on one of his visits to Delhi, he was able to gain access to Rashtrapati Bhavan, to visit the exact place where he, as a young lad, stood with his mother, to collect the Ashoka Chakra Award (posthumous).

The story has a special meaning for me because the guard of that train was my grandfather, Benny Calvert. My father Ron tells me that Johannes, who was terribly burnt, went up to my grandfather and slumped against him. Benny's spotless white guard's uniform was imprinted with the contours of Mack's charred hands. My grandfather kept that uniform for many years as a grim reminder of the ultimate sacrifice of his brave colleague.

Lillooah Revisited
Memories of 1940s

Denis K. Whitworth

A close-knit Railway settlement some four miles outside the city of Calcutta in India, Lillooah was basically home to the European and Anglo-Indian families of staff who were employed by the Railway in their Carriage & Wagon Workshops. In the late 1930s, when I was privileged to be appointed as an Apprentice Engineer, I found the colony contained only three main roads within the confines of its limited boundaries. The sole entrance to this private residential area was approached from the Grand Trunk Road, and it was permanently manned by a member of the Watch & Ward Department who was under strict orders to raise the entrance barrier only to authorised personnel.

True to the tradition of class distinction during those days of British rule, there was a definite purpose in the planning of the three roads that ran parallel to one another in the colony. The first, Gardiner Road, was a beautiful tree-lined thoroughfare, arboured for the most part, with resplendent mansions on either side. Every building boasted luxuriant, well-cared-for gardens that advertised the status and obvious opulence of the occupants who were the officers.

The second road, Pearce Road, was centrally located within the colony, and contained blocks of houses on both sides that were occupied by the "middle rank" of the hierarchy. These were the Workshop Foremen, Assistant Foremen and Senior Chargemen. One building however, was designed to serve as a Nursery Day School for the children of Railway staff, and many hundreds of them started their academic careers under the watchful and professional eyes of the headmistress Kitty David and her assistant Flora MacDonald.

Lillooah railway station in the '40s

The third road, Jenyns Road, had high-rise blocks containing multiple living quarters, and one in particular No. 41, housed as many as fifteen families! Most of the occupants on the road were the "lower grade" staff, chargemen, charge hands and apprentice engineers who had not been long enough in service to warrant better accommodation.

Buildings along the length of Jenyns Road were located on one side only, as the other side, for the most part, overlooked grassland where hockey, football and other sporting events were held. The area was also used for the Workshop's Annual Sports Day meetings.

Three buildings on the road were reserved for specific purposes. The Watch & Ward and Railway Protection Police operated from one, which also served as the Armoury, Miniature Rifle Range and A.F.(I) Training Centre. The second building was used by the Medical Officer as a Surgery and temporary Hospital, and the third was converted into a Hostel to house the apprentice engineers who were selected, each year, to supplement the need for trained supervisors within the Industry.

Standing: "Birdie" Wilton, Norma Marshal, George D'Coster, Arthur Daniell, Victor Wilton, Gladys Hart & Sheila Culpepper. Seated: Gillian D'Coster, Rena Peters, Gloria Preston, Sybil Pinto, Doris D'Coster, Marie Daniell & Dennis Culpepper.

Immediately opposite the Hostel was the Lillooah Post Office where, no doubt, many a letter was posted from homesick lads who had left the security and comfort of their homes for the first time...

Alongside the Post Office, and on the opposite side of the existing minor roadway, the Workshop's imposing iron gates could be seen. Through them, only staff resident in the colony were permitted to pass on their way to their various job stations. It was noticeable that the Indian workmen were accorded a separate entrance, and not permitted access through the main iron gates.

Mary Daniels, Doris Pinto, Marjorie Daly and Mary Gentry enjoy a dip in the swimming pool.

Within the boundaries of the colony, there was a large pool which was more commonly referred to as "The Tank!" Much of the Tank was congested with weeds which made swimming in it a hazard, and rumour had it that more than one person had drowned in its murky depths, trapped under by the density of the undergrowth.

On the bright side, however, many a fish was caught by some of the colony's eager anglers. Names of those avid fishermen that come to my mind are Bill Smith, Harry Halden, 'Baldy' Hearne, Jim Robinson and Neil Corbett.

The swimming pool was a new feature in the mid-1940s, and it was located at the residential end of the Tank. Many an enjoyable gala was held at the poolside, and many an enjoyable swim was taken in those cool waters during long, endless summer days. How well I remember Maureen Morgan's amazing prowess in the water! Her ability to swim lap after lap put my maximum lap and a half to shame, and I discreetly avoided the pool whenever she was there.

The Church within the colony was for Anglican worshippers, and Roman Catholics had to leave the colony to walk a short distance down the Grand Trunk Road before turning on to a dirt track for about 500 yards where the new Don Bosco Church was located.

Denis and Sybil Whitworth

Last, but by no means least, the Railway Institute! This red-bricked edifice was the focal point and meeting place of residents throughout the year. It was located on the opposite side of the Tank to that on which the swimming pool was sited.

A short distance away from the Institute, and approached by an overhead bridge, was the Lillooah Railway Station from where regular journeys into Calcutta, via Howrah Station, were taken. The four-mile run took us from the relative peace and serenity of a colony into a city teeming with throngs, traffic, trams, taxis and tongas ... a world in direct contrast to Lillooah! Nevertheless, every one of us took great pleasure in visiting "the great city", a city that was comparatively clean compared with how we understand it is today. Of particular interest to us were shopping sprees at the famous New Market and the parade of fabulous shops in Chowringhee and in the Esplanade. Cinema shows at the "Metro", "Lighthouse", "Odeon", "Plaza" and other picture houses were second to none. I can still sense the aroma and atmosphere within the air-conditioned, thickly-carpeted, soundproof interiors of the first two named cinemas, and I will always associate the "Metro" with Rhett Butler's famous words to a sobbing Scarlett O'Hara: "Frankly, my dear, I don't give a damn!"

With the grandeur of India's one-time capital so near at hand, however, Lillooah can be proud that most of its residents were content to remain in the comfort of a private colony, within a close-knit and caring community, and in the knowledge that all their entertainment requirements were available within "a stone's throw" of their homes. The Institute offered a lot more than Calcutta did!

Yes, life in Lillooah during the 1930s, '40s and '50s – certainly during my stay there – could not have been happier.

Photographs courtesy: Denis K. Whitworth

This article was first published in The National Anglo-Indian Railway Convention Souvenir 2003, edited by Dr. Beatrix D'Souza

THE MADURAI RAILWAY INSTITUTE

Sydney J. Ellis

I SIMPLY CAN'T forget the 195Øs and 196Øs in Madurai, especially the functions at the Railway Institute. Whenever we meet at dinner dances, curry nights or even small parties in Melbourne, we AIs can't help reminiscing about those times, the fun we had and the unforgettable memories of the Madurai Railway Institute.

The Institute was opposite the Anglican Church of Divine Patience and just a 10-minute walk from the Catholic Sacred Heart Railway Colony Church. Weddings at either of these churches were usually at 5 p.m. followed by receptions at the Institute. The bride and groom invariably turned up at about 6.30 (after photo shoots at studios) and the receptions commenced with a noisy and colourful welcome to the bridal couple, bridesmaids, groomsmen, flower girl and page boy. The grand march was more often than not right around the outside of the Institute and back indoors. In those days there were no tables inside the hall.

Everybody enjoyed themselves and sometimes the receptions lasted until 3 a.m. even though the refreshments ran out long before that. The guests just wanted to dance the night away. I recall emceeing Anto and Aureen Patterson's wedding in the '60s when the guests refused to leave until 5 a.m.!

In the early '60s prohibition was in force; however, some liquor was smuggled from Kerala and some "home-made" stuff was also available. At dances, some of which I emceed, when I announced the first dance, only a few would get up and dance with their wives or girlfriends, but after a round of drinks, the hall would be packed with dancers. The illicit drinks sure packed a punch full of courage.

Madurai Railway Institute, Tamil Nadu, South India

However, by about midnight, the four billiard tables in the billiard room were used as beds for a number of chaps all blissfully unaware of where they were.

The "Tag" and "Paul Jones" dances were a treat.

Sometimes when a boy had a tiff with his girlfriend and knew she would refuse to dance with him if he asked her to, he would come to the stage and plead with me to announce a "Paul Jones" and to ask my assistant to stop the music at precisely the time he was opposite her.

My assistant, Raymond Sharpe who looked after the music and who was adept at this would oblige. Many a couple made up this way.

The slow foxtrots and twilight dances provided the romantic atmosphere and the music for many couples to dance close to each other.

It was amusing to see anxious mothers trying to peer through the dimmed lights to see their daughters. I think many serious relationships started at these dances and climaxed at the altar.

Sometimes there were fights at these dances. Fortunately these were few and far between and the sober adults soon evicted the quarrelsome and, more often than not, drunken young chaps.

At one of these occasions one chap who worked as a fitter in the loco shed dressed as a leper and sat at the entrance of the Institute with a bowl in front of him. He looked filthy and had painted his face and hands so well that he looked like a real leper. No one recognised him and many complained that he should be removed. Instead, he wandered into the hall and sat on the floor in the middle of the hall. I cannot forget the shock and horror on the faces of the people. He winked at someone who recognised him. Word soon spread that he was Maurice Julee and the howls of laughter that followed will remain in my memory forever.

At another function a lovely girl, Dimpy Freer, came dressed as Cleopatra complete with a couple of slaves with large fans. She was a sight to behold and not surprisingly walked away with the first prize.

In 1967 we spent our last Christmas in Madurai before emigrating to Australia. The All-India Anglo-Indian Association (Madurai Branch) organised the Christmas dance. It was the last dance I emceed...

Photo courtesy: Sydney J. Ellis

Mumbai's Last Anglo-Indian Motorman

Roana Costa

Adrian Eric Baldrey was the last Anglo-Indian motorman on the Mumbai suburban railway network. He belongs to the fading Anglo-Indian community that once ran the Indian Railways.

Baldrey's father Eric George Baldrey was a mail driver on the Bhusaval route and his grandfather George Singleton Baldrey a mail driver on the old steam locomotives. Both worked for the Great Indian Peninsular Railway. Baldrey's brothers work in technical maintenance at the locomotive sheds and his father-in-law was a rail driver in the Jhansi division. Like his, other Anglo-Indian families held responsible positions in the gigantic railway system and some of them had surnames which reflected their vocation, such as Caboose (a guard's van).

V. Anand, former Southern Railway general manager, wrote an article on the occasion of the National Anglo-Indian Railway Convention in 2003, praising the community for their skills as locomotive drivers. He said their pride and workmanship was incomparable . "It is sad that with the migration of Anglo-Indians to Canada and Australia, their numbers have dwindled. Everyone has only pleasant things to say about this community. In fact, I have never met a dishonest Anglo," he says.

Baldrey's earliest memories are of the railway quarters at Bhusaval, a far cry from his 1BHK apartment in Kalyan which he shares with his mother and brother's family. "Our cottage in Bhusaval was beautiful. We had a farm with 30 goats, fowl, geese and orchards with the tastiest mangoes and plums. Mum really misses those days. She compares our flat here to matchboxes," he says with a dreamy look in his green-grey eyes. "We lived at D2-44. My oldest sister got married from that house. The grey cottage with its high ceiling and skylights, huge rooms and halls, chimney and fireplace is etched in my memory."

Mumbai Motorman Adrian Baldrey on his last run.

Growing up amidst railway officers and their tales of adventure, it was hardly surprising that Baldrey was fascinated by trains. To quench his curiosity, he accompanied his father on many of his trips. "I was around 14 years old but had the advantage of good height and build," says the motorman who is over 6 ft tall. With his strapping physique, beard and shock of hair he cuts quite a figure. "I used to disguise myself as a fireman by tying the customary handkerchief around my head or donning a felt cap," he says with a mischievous grin.

Hanging around with his dad was an education in itself since Baldrey's father had a chance to operate all three types of trains: steam, diesel, and during the last five years of his career, electric rakes. "Dad had his own steam engine with his name engraved on a plate," says the 56-year-old bachelor who himself has an impressive 34-year career behind him. He started out as an assistant driver in 1974, graduated to a goods train driver and for the last 19 years has been a suburban motorman.

A Mumbai motorman's job can be brutal. "The first time I ran over a woman was when I was an assistant driver," he says. "I was on the Lonavla-Pune track when I saw a middle-aged woman crossing at the bend. I honked and blew the whistle but..."

He continues, "Like every other motorman, I cleared the tracks with my bare hands out of respect for the dead. Accidents are a job hazard and with time you get seasoned. But there are days when an old memory can still make me lose my appetite."

That's when Baldrey turns to M. Desa, senior loco inspector, who counsels motormen going through stress and mild trauma. "People don't understand why a train is late and always think it's the motorman's fault. I am Baldrey's friend, philosopher and guide, both in his personal and professional life," says Desa, who was once a motorman himself.

Baldrey has many tales to tell. He animatedly describes how he saved a life by accurate judgment and shudders when he describes the 26/7 deluge when he was chest deep in water for two days but refused to leave his rake.

"I survived on water, vada pav and biscuits," he says. "There are good days, there are bad days and there are great days. I took them as they came. All I can say is that my life has been an adventurous journey and I have enjoyed the ride."

Article / Photo courtesy: The Times of India

Villupuram

Cheryl-Ann Shivan

Villupuram, a railway junction around 16Ø kms from Madras, was once a famous Anglo-Indian hub in the South of India.

Built in 1905 as a recreational center for British and Anglo-Indian railway people, the Villupuram Railway Institute was a place where they could come in for a game of cards or a game of billiards, or just relax and chat with friends over a cup of coffee or a cold drink; and then at special times they could congregate for dances or hold tennis matches on its lawns. The Institute has continued over the last ten decades to fulfill the very purpose for which it was first constructed.

The grand old men and women of Villupuram recall with wet-eyed nostalgia the very many personal family celebrations and dances that took place at the Institute. With a very faraway look in their eyes they describe the excitement of getting dressed in candle light or under petromax lanterns! Those were the days when "Lounge" or "Dress Suits Essential" was to be found on the invitations announcing the dances. Brass bands like the Daniel's or the Gabriel's were booked to play; "Under the Spreading Chestnut Tree" was a favourite tune to which the dancers would arrange themselves in a particular fashion and then gesticulate to the words being sung, not unlike the way today's youth dance to "Macarina" and the "Ketchup Song". The MCs were made up of sterner stuff and if they felt a quarrel brewing, the trouble makers were marched out onto the grounds to work out their differences and the band would strike up again to draw attention away from what was going on outside. Decorum, on all fronts, was strictly maintained.

Villupuram Railway Institute, 1950

The next generation grew up and danced to the tunes of the Hubert Gorman and Alfie Pinto bands. They remember the week-long Christmas functions that started on the 23rd of December and ended on the 1st of the New Year. Unfortunately the Christmas week celebrations slowly came to an end in the late '60s and early '70s when the Anglo-Indian population started migrating overseas and paucity of funds discouraged such extensive dos. However, the Christmas and New Year dances continued to be held and bands from Trichy, Madurai and Madras were booked to provide the music.

Anglo-Indians in the '70s, '80s, and early '90s listened and danced to the tunes of "The Trend Setters", "The Evil

Blends" and the very popular and probably the most enduring "Purple Haze". Local bands in Villupuram had enough talent to keep the crowds from Madras, Trichy, Madurai and Pondicherry entertained. Those were the days when there were more people than dancing space allowed. This however was not regretted by many of the couples as it gave them an excuse to dance cheek to cheek! Everyone remembers The May Queen Ball in the late '60s and early '70s and the heated competition and rivalry that it evoked among all the lovely ladies in the hall.

The latter half of the '90s saw the introduction of disc jockeys with their boxes of different kinds of music, who proved more economical for the organisers, but who could in no way ever replace the excitement of a live band. Today, disc jockeys have come to stay and the present generation, according to the senior citizens, are witness to only a shade of the entertainment of the yesteryears.

The institute has not only lent itself for occasions like the dances and Christmas celebrations but has endorsed numerous love stories and happy endings. In a recently administered questionnaire to Anglo-Indians from Villupuram and Pondicherry, as part of a research programme on the Community, several answered the question: "Where did you meet your spouse?" with "On the dance floor of the Railway Institute in Villupuram."

Two stern black and white photographs of the European gentlemen (unfortunately nobody can put names to them) on the walls of the Institute seem to be calling out for a maintenance of old standards. But the recently added, much smaller colour photograph of late Irudhayam, the former marker at the Institute, is a poignant reminder that the "old order changed, yielding place to the new." Today, Anglo-Indian celebrations in Villupuram are few and far between and the drastic reduction in the number of families living in this town has resulted in the fall in attendance. Some families that had formerly lived in Villupuram and who still cherish memories of their lives there make the effort to occasionally return from neighbouring Pondicherry and Madras to attend a Social or a Dance. They bring with them their children hoping they will be able to experience something of the old times.

Photo courtesy: Cheryl-Ann Shivan

A Tiger on the Track

Dorothy Sherman

My Dad Robert "Bob" Shea was a railwayman from the age of 17 and he retired at age 55. He started his career on the BNR as a guard and finished as Traffic Inspector, Bilaspur. My two younger sisters and I had many happy years growing up in several railway stations. My earliest recollections are from places called Khurda Road and Kantabanji.

This article is a very early memory of an episode that occurred in Kantabanji. Recalling it now enchants and thrills me, even though it happened more than half a century ago. My Dad would take great delight in relating it over and over again to us girls, just to see the look on our faces.

Our childhood was full of experiences, too many to document at this time, but one stands out in particular and has stayed with me, indelibly stamped in my memory...

Dad had a long time 'Shikari' (Indian hunter) friend named Mr. Primm. He was a permanent way inspector (P.W.I.) on the railway line which ran through Kantabanji and he was also a very ardent collector of animal skins. I remember, as a little girl walking around his home with my sisters, gazing in fear and awe at all the tiger and leopard skins complete with heads mounted on walls and in front of the fireplace. Dad would tease us and place his hand on the mouth of the tiger and we'd scream in terror even though we knew the tiger was long deceased and his beautiful brandy coloured eyes were simply made of glass marbles to make his head look life like. Mr. Primm had a beautiful and only daughter named Bridget, who was 18 years old (not at all in our league), but she played games with us, told us stories of the experiences with her father's hunting expeditions and thrilled us no end, whenever we visited with our parents.

We were fortunate enough to be invited to many a small game hunt which was considered safe for little kids and though saddened by the shooting of little foxes, peacocks and deer, we liked riding in the backs of lorry trucks and climbing up into the 'Machans' (tree platfarms) built high up in the trees to watch the jungle from a safe height. It was to one such shooting expedition that Mr. Primm and his daughter Bridget invited my parents. It was to have been a peacock shoot, so only 12 bore rifles (low powered) were taken along.

The group left Kantabanji railway station at around 5 p.m. on a railway trolley. It was a little platform of wooden slats, with two benches similar to park benches with wooden slats, a wide umbrella, and had 4 wheels like those of a railway carriage. It travelled totally on push power. There were two Indian men who knew the jungle and the railway track well and they used two manual levers attached to each back wheel to push the trolley along the railway track.

Illustrations: Harry MacLure

Mr. Primm and Bridget sat in the front seat and my Mum Louise and Dad on the seat behind them. Once the trolley gained momentum after being pushed for a few minutes, the trolley-men jumped on and the trolley would cruise along at a fair speed for several miles. When it slowed down the natives would jump off and repeat the push procedure again. Later on they would use motorised trollies, but this was the early 1950s and only manual ones were in use then. My Granny and ayah stood with my sisters and me, sadly waving good bye to Mum and Dad as they departed the Kantabanji platform with the Primms and trolley-men.

The trolley cruised and slowed, cruised and slowed, on and on for several miles. My parents noticed it was getting dark and the vegetation on the side of the side of the railway tracks was changing from clumps of bamboo, tall grasses and thickets, into dark and thick jungle foliage. One of the trolley-men spotted something sitting on the side of the tracks in the distance and shouted *"Sher, Saab, Sher!"* (Tiger, Sir, Tiger!).

Mr. Primm ordered the men to get closer and picked up his 12 bore rifle getting the tiger in his sights. The trolley-men stopped the trolley only a few yards away from one of the most majestic beasts they had ever seen. It was a young tigress in her prime. She sat fully composed surveying the group casually, almost as if deciding who she should devour first. Dad said he was transfixed with fear as he sat closest to the tiger. If she had decided to kill, Dad would have been her first victim. I cried when he told us this and to this day I get a little chill running down my spine when I think about how close I came to losing my beloved parents. They were so close to a tiger in the wild, in its very own habitat. They said her colouring took their breath away. She had broad almost deep burgundy coloured stripes on the deepest yellow gold background. Her tail was long and elegant and swished from side to side. The muscles of her strong body rippled with each movement she made. Her large brandy ball eyes were so close you could almost see the dark pupils as she stared.

Mr. Primm declared he would like to have a shot at the tiger, but wasn't sure he could kill her with his first shot. Bridget tried her best to dissuade her father. He raved about the tiger's beautiful skin; he could almost see it displayed on the wall of his living room and said it would fetch a handsome first prize at the Shikari club. Bridget was pleading with her father not to shoot. Mum 'joined in the argument' and said he wasn't to even try because he had them all with him and the risk was too great. The trolley-men felt if Mr. Primm missed his shot, the angry tiger would kill them all. Maybe they should come back another day for the prize. Throughout the debate, Dad sat still as if he was carved in stone, not even daring to move a muscle. The tiger just yawned, got up gingerly swishing her tail and walked slowly and majestically away beside the track and down into the jungle. She turned a last time and gave a great roar as if to warn them not to follow her. The trolley-men said she would have attacked, but for her cubs nearby. Mr. Primm stood up in disgust, stamping his foot, muttering that he had missed the chance of a lifetime, all because of the rest of the crew. The 'peacock shoot' came to an abrupt end. The trolley men turned the trolley around and brought home a very disgruntled Shikari and a relieved Mum and Dad to their waiting family.

Granny declared she had sent their guardian angels and that was the only reason they had returned safely. In the next couple years, I saw many a new and prized tiger skin appear on Mr. Primm's sitting room walls and often wondered if one of them belonged to our 'Sher ki Rani' (Tiger Queen).

NOEL 'BULLY' NETTO
THE DANCING DRIVER

Harry MacLure

BULLY NETTO WAS a superfast Special 'A' grade driver on the M&SM (Southern) Railway. He now lives a retired life in Chennai. Even though his "running life" took up most of his time, Bully always made it a point to shelve his free periods for his all-time passion – dancing.

Bully Netto

Born in Madras in 1927 to Albert and Irene Netto (née Garrett), Bully studied at the Pudupet Convent and later at St. Mary's. He was appointed as an 'A' grade fireman in 1945 on a salary of Rs. 40 per month. In 1954, he married Yvonne

Claire Jones, who has since passed on. They were blessed with 14 children – 9 daughters and 5 sons.

Bully in action with one of his daughters

All his daughters had the privilege of dancing the Tango with Bully.

At a young age Bully learned to dance at the Perambur Railway Institute in those days when dancing was a stylish art form, before disco "writhing" took over.

His transfer to Jolarpet Junction, 90 miles from Bangalore, helped Bully to further hone his dancing skills. Bangalore was teeming with Anglo-Indian bands playing great music. Bully won several competitions in Chennai, Calcutta, Bangalore and Bombay. His earliest partner was Theresa

Gomes. And later, of course, his wife Yvonne became his dancing partner.

Bully had a good railway track record. He retired in 1975 and now lives in Chennai after 40 years of accident-free service, and has received many commendations for his meritorious and loyal contribution to the railways.

He had worked very hard for his family and has been a good father to his children. His contribution to the Anglo-Indian dance circuit is much more than has been recognized. He has that rare distinction of having shaped his dancing style on his own terms, all the while excelling in the very demanding profession of being a railway locomotive driver.

Photo courtesy: Noel 'Bully' Netto

Fr. Bernard Caszo, MSFS
From Engineman to Man of God

Warren Caszo

Aloysius Bernard Caszo, eldest son of Lawrence Reginald Caszo and Dorothy Caszo (née Walsh), was born in Rajahmundry in 1932. He first studied in the local railway school and then passed the High School Examination from St. Bede's, Madras, 1949.

When did Bernard first hear the Divine Call? Most probably when, as a 15-year-old, he was afflicted with an ailment diagnosed as potentially fatal. Dad Reggie walked across the river Godavari several times to buy the life-saving drug, available only at Kovvur on the other side of the famous bridge. His parents stormed the heavens and Bernard was cured. Reggie told his son that God had saved him for a higher purpose; Bernard believed this, so did Fr. John Lawrence, the erstwhile parish priest of RJY, who very keenly observed, nurtured and monitored Bernard's vocation.

A shy, handsome teenager who looked like Tony Curtis, Bernard was also an athlete with soccer and hockey skills. Needless to add, the young lad had many female admirers. As though his impenetrable reserve was not defence enough, Bernard even grew a bushy beard to keep the fair sex at bay!

Just ordained : Fr. Bernard Caszo, MSFS, as a young priest

The Caszos were a family of ten. Dad Reggie, a driver, was the sole breadwinner. As the eldest son, Bernard took it upon himself to help make both ends meet. In 1950, the 18-year-old began to heave and shovel coal in the steam locomotives.

He was an A-grade fireman in Rajahmundry, Southern Railway. Firing was strenuous and hazardous, especially "picking up line-clear at a train speed of 100 kmph. He performed this gruelling task well and in 1957, at 25, was the youngest driver on the Southern Railway, with rosy career prospects. Yet, above the hiss of steam, the clank of couplings, the sound of train on track, Bernard could still hear the persistent call from above. Deeply religious, even after a hard night's trip, Bernard used to make it for morning Mass. Off duty, he spent long hours alone in the church in silent prayer.

Fr. Bernard Caszo, MSFS, now

The very same year, with the consent of his parents and the guidance of Fr. Lawrence, Bishop Baud and Bishop Eugene

D'Souza, Bernard gave up his railway job to join the seminary at Nagpur. He was sent to Fribourg, Switzerland, for further studies, receiving Holy Orders there on 17th March 1957. Shortly after, he returned to India to say his first Mass in the church of St. Joan of Arc, Rajahmundry, an event of joy and pride for the Caszo family, relatives and friends. Since then, Fr. Bernard has officiated at family functions, weddings, christenings and other religious ceremonies. He is loved and respected by his many neices and nephews.

He belongs to the order of the Missionaries of St. Francis de Sales. While serving in St. Aloysius High School, Vizag, he helped many Anglo-Indian boys with tuition fees, books and uniforms. He has taught seminarians in Kottayam, Kerala, and Anantapur, Andhra Pradesh.

His tenure as Parish Priest of St. Joseph's Parish Waltair in the '80s, will be remembered for the construction of a parish hall, a crying need of the parishioners especially the youth. It stands today as a memorial to his concern for his flock. His short and sweet sermons and melodious voice added special flavour and fervour to the parish services.

In 1989, he opted to serve overseas and was the parish priest of Devizes, UK, for 14 years. He is presently Chaplain to the Sisters of Mercy, St. Michael's Convent, Clacton-on-Sea, Essex, UK. His lively spirit has not waned with age, but after 81 summers, there is some physical wear and tear. The good sisters look after him tenderly.

Fr. Bernard is fondly remembered by the Anglo-Indian community in Vizag and Rajahmundry, his many former parishioners, relatives and friends in the UK, USA and Australia. He continues to support seminarians in Vizag through donations.

Photographs courtesy: Warren Caszo

The Godavari Floods of 1953

The whole of Rajahmundry was under 10ft of water. This photo was taken during the mighty Godavari floods of 1953. Anglo-Indians where given a coupé per family and we stayed on the train for nearly a fortnight moving from station to station as per the Railways safety warnings. I am in the center (G.E. Waring) the tallest amongst the children.

For us children we did not realize the danger of the calamity. It was like a picnic and a circus. Anglo-Indians those days had big families with an added family of pets. So there were dogs, cats, monkeys, goats, parrots, mynahs, pigeons, love birds, rabbits, fish, pigs and even a spotted deer! You could call it Noah's Ark. And then there was this spruce Anglo-Indian lady of over 90 years who insisted on bringing her cow along or she was not boarding the train. Needless to add, the Railways gave in to her...

Text and Photograph: G.E. Waring

Three Colonies and a Community

Trevor Rosemeyer

Tundla is almost 25 kms east of Agra. It still is a very busy railway junction. Trains moving towards Kanpur, Allahabad, Lucknow, Mughalsarai, Patna, Calcutta and beyond have to pass through this busy station.

Front view of Christ Church, Tundla.

Photo courtesy: Trevor Rosemeyer

However, today Tundla is just a shadow of its glorious Anglo-Indian past. Nearly every railway bungalow housed an Anglo-Indian family. The railway Institute outside the station, hosted some of the most famous dances in the past. Today it lies locked up with myriads of memories, dilapidated and forlorn. Anglo-Indians from far and near, from places like Jhansi, Kanpur, Allahabad and Lucknow travelled the distance just to attend these shows.

The old abandoned Railway Institute, Tundla.

Photo courtesy: Trevor Rosemeyer

The quaint little church outside the station entrance bears almost a deserted look now. Perhaps each edifice could tell a story of its own. Like all things else, this once serene colony has seen its share of development take place transforming the earlier landscape. The sounds of trains still reverberate, but not the steam engines.Only three Anglo-Indian families remain in this once bustling Anglo-Indian settlement – the Woodwards, the Vanderverts and the McCurtis'. They are the last of the breed in what was once a big Anglo-Indian colony.

* * *

BANDIKUI, IN RAJASTHAN, was also once filled with Anglo-Indians. It lies on the branch line between Bharatpur and Jaipur about 160 kms from Agra. It was once part of the Bombay Baroda and Central India Railway, now better known as North West Railway. Its importance lay in the large loco shed that provided engines for all trains.

Bandikui Railway Station

Photo courtesy: Nigel Foote

Bandikui was also a crew changing stop. It was famous for its senior Institute meant exclusively for the Europeans and Anglo-Indians, and for its bowling green. The Christmas functions once held here were as good as they get in any other place. An annual bowling competition used to be held here. Among the other pleasures in which our fellow Anglo-Indians used to indulge were fishing and shooting in the surrounding Aravalli hills and Salash river. Some of the renowned Anglo-Indian train drivers hailing from this place were Archibald Betram Carr, Jeffrey Boles, Alex Joseph, E.D. Carr, Kelvin

Quieros, Mr. Phillips and Mr. Lobo. Among the guards there were Mr. C. Johnson, Mr. C. Rose and Mr. Owen Rose. Sadly there are no more Anglo-Indian families residing here.

Bandikui European Institute

Photo courtesy: Nigel Foote

One of the most famous incidents to have occurred here long time ago was the visit of Queen Elizabeth. She was taken from here by a special train to the Ranthambore Tiger Sanctuary. The crew of that train was exclusively Anglo-Indian – the driver was Archibald Carr, the guard was Cyril Jordan. The pilot engine was driven by Jeffrey Boles. After the trip, the Queen was highly impressed so she met the driver and the guard and posed with them for a photograph. As a token of thanksgiving, on her return to England, she sent each one of them a letter of appreciation and a large-size photograph with them. Something to cherish for posterity.

Joan Quieros and Brian Robbins outside the Quieros' bungalow

Photo courtesy: Andrew Quieros

On another occasion, a GM special train was run from Ahmedabad to Delhi. The General Manager wanted to know who the driver was. It so happened that the driver was none other than Oswlad F. Carr, better known as 'Speedster Carr'. The crew changed at Jaipur and this time the driver was Archibald Carr. On hearing this, the curious G.M. remarked, "Is this a Carr Special?" Archibald, also known as Mr. Rulebook, once remarked, "I am paid to keep the time, not to make up lost time." Such was the quality of those Anglo-Indian drivers!

* * *

GANGAPUR CITY WAS another famous old Anglo-Indian hub. It is located between Bharatpur and Sawai Madhopur in Rajasthan, about 160 kms from Agra. It also used to be part of the Bombay Baroda and Central India Railway, now rechristened North Central Railway. Gangapur used to be a serene, small railway colony famous for its huge loco shed where engines for all kinds of trains were maintained.

Christmas was always celebrated in a special way here. Phillip Carville, to whom I am deeply indebted for much of this information, remembers clearly the days when his band from Agra would go to Gangapur and serenade the night away at many of the shows. He remembers well the many romances which blossomed there between the Gangapur belles and the Agra beaus. He tells me that many of the dances invariably ended up in fisticuffs over the local beauties. However, the matter was always resolved in an amicable manner behind the Institute under the strict supervision of some elders. Phillip Carville was perhaps the last Anglo-Indian guard to work on this route, his last assignment being on the New Delhi-Mumbai Rajdhani Express.

Some of the other great Anglo-Indian train drivers and guards from Gangapur were J.B. Leyton, George Harris, R.R. Franklin, R.R. Weston, F. Weston, Charlie Critchell, Mr. Puttman, Mr. Lewis, Mr. Middlecoat, W.R. Stewart, C. Williams, Fred Gillespie, Trevor Bouvard and E.K. Shemain. Mr. Archie Williams had the honour of being the station master. The loco inspectors were Tony Franklin and E.J. Loveday.

As Gangapur did not have any proper schools, most of the Anglo-Indian children studied at St. Peter's College and St. Patrick's Convent in Agra. Sadly, there are no more Anglo-Indian families in Gangapur City. All that remains are memories and stories of 'Sahibs and Memsahibs'.

The Fullers
Five Generations of Railwaymen

Harry MacLure

Norman Anthony Fuller, an Anglo-Indian now settled in Florida, has been responsible for drawing up the Fuller family tree dating back to around 1815. He contacted relatives and friends residing in various countries, visited archives where information regarding births, deaths and marriages of Anglo-Indians in India was stored on microfilm. His younger brother, Patrick Beresford Fuller, resident of Madras, visited numerous churches and cemeteries in South India to add to the information, all of which is supported by certificates. Today, the family tree consists of 81 printed pages!

Of particular note is that of the seven generations of Fullers, commencing with Thomas and Lydia Fuller, who have been traced, five generations have been employed by the railways — the 2nd, 3rd, 4th and 5th generations as drivers and the 6th in other railway employment with the Southern Railway. Many members of Lydia's family were also in the railways.

The saga of the Fuller family began in c.1815 with Thomas and Lydia Fuller of Coimbatore. The Fullers grew with links in the Figredo, Lopez, Narcis, Laporte, Dennis, Watkins and Stephenson families.

Photograph taken in Madurai, South India, 1917. Ellen Matilda Fuller (neé Narcis), wife of Albert James Fuller who died in 1906 at Asansol, with their five children: Ada, Bertie, Ozzie, Josphine and Edgar Fuller. (This is the only known surviving photograph of Ellen Matilda Fuller)

In August 1838, John Edward Fuller was born to Thomas and Lydia. In October 1864, he became an engine driver of the Madras Railway Company, headquartered in Royapuram. He married Maria Cronan. Their son, Albert James Fuller, was born in September 1866 in Madras. He was employed in Madura (now Madurai) as a fireman and married Ellen Narcis in 1889. Four of his children were born in Madura. In 1902 he moved to Asansol in Bengal to work as a shunting driver, and it was here in Asansol between 1902 and 1906 his sons John Burton and Oswald attended school at North Point in Darjeeling.

When Albert James Fuller died suddenly in 1906, the sons were taken out of North Point School, Darjeeling, and the family moved back to Madura. The elder boy, John Burton Fuller, started working as a fireman at the age of 15 and in time became a Grade A Driver. He was 26 years old when he married Mary Mildred Constance Stephenson in September 1921. Mary Mildred was a trained teacher from St. Columban's, Madras, and taught in the Railway School, Madura.

The Fullers at a family reunion in Chennai

John Burton Fuller, three years after the death of his wife, married again in 1935. He was appointed Loco Inspector, Podanur, and retired as Loco Foreman, Calicut.

Patrick Beresford Fuller
Electric Train Driver

John Burton and Mary Mildred Fuller's son Patrick Beresford Fuller, was born in February 1931 and married Noveen Josephine Lavocah in June 1953. He entered Railway service as an apprentice mechanic, South India Railway Central Workshops, Golden Rock, transferred to Tambaram where he became an Electric Train Driver in 1956, and then transferred to Egmore as Mail/Express Driver and voluntarily retired from the Railways in 1988 after having served for 32 years; during which he was awarded various awards including a citation for 20 years of accident free driving, and cash prizes in recognition of his meritorious service.

Noel Fuller at the Egmore Railway Station on the last run of the Meter Gauge Train, 2004

Noel Everad Fuller, son of Patrick Beresford Fuller, now constitute the family's sixth generation connections with the Railways. He was born in November 1959, joined Southern Railway in 1981 and is a Technician I in the EMU and AC loco workshop, Tambaram.

The Fullers' family link with the Railways which has been an unbroken tradition for the past 158 years since 1856 will sadly be ending with Noel Fuller as his two sons have opted to move on and away from the Railways: Denzil completed his B.Tech. Marine Engineering and is now sailing as 4th Engineer and Andrew the second boy completed his B.E. Computer Engineering and is undergoing training at the Officer's Training Academy in Madras as a Commissioned Officer in the Indian Army.

Photographs courtesy: The Fuller family

Anglo-Indians
Loyal Workers or Good Soldiers?

Noel Thomas

At a recent book launch of the Anglo-Ink publishing company in Madras, I heard a speaker say that Anglo-Indians never joined a strike. Another speaker was quick to differ, pointing out that one of the first strikes in Madras was led by an Anglo-Indian.

The first statement is a widely accepted generalisation, a characteristic of the favourite Anglo-Indian stereotype.

However, both statements brought back to my mind many firsthand experiences during my forty odd years of railway service in both the subordinate and the gazetted cadres.

Writing from both sides of the fence, I can say that while most Anglo-Indians shunned the very thought of going on strike, there were a few who felt no compunctions in breaking free from the traditional community mindset. When I joined the Railways in the late '50s, there were 3 main labour unions: leftist, rightist and centrist. The unions enjoyed political patronage. With a few exceptions, union leaders belonged to some political party or other.

As a rule an Anglo-Indian never joined a union. He was a good soldier, ingrained with a sense of military discipline through heritage, upbringing and education. He saw the unionist as a potential striker, so joining a union was an embarrassment for him. "Please don't ask me to join. Ask me anything else" was his attitude. Taking part in a demonstration, inciting others to go slow, all this was anathema to the Anglo-Indian. The engines, the trains, the tracks, the platforms, were all part of the Anglo-Indian identity – keeping the wheels moving was his *raison d'etre.* His work was meat and drink for him. Anyone trying to put a spoke in the wheels was a traitor, a fifth columnist, a commie. Slogans like: *"Chakka Bandh Karo"* and *"Inquilab Zindabad"* infuriated him. He was a soldier from his roots; to revolt was alien to his being. The first commandment for an Anglo-Indian railway recruit was "Thou shalt not strike!"

Thus, the railway administration was assured of the loyalty of its Anglo-Indian employees. This loyalty was also rewarded at times. Anglo-Indian volunteers were quickly absorbed into the regular workforce. They started their career under obligation to wear their loyalty on their sleeves. Anglo-Indians were preferred for promotion to the "running" categories which kept the wheels moving.

The AFI and Territorial Army units, with a fair complement of AIs, were effectively utilised to break strikes.

His colleagues from other Indian communities respected the Anglo-Indian for his work ethic of hard work and fair-mindedness, but in their perception, what alienated him was his "blinkered attitude" and refusal to join hands with them for a just common cause. It was this betrayal which rankled with them. They could not understand his mindset, his soldierly obedience to the commander, British or Indian (Railway boss). The bosses understood this and exploited it to the hilt.

It is not my case that Anglo-Indian workers should have plunged headlong and indiscriminately into the labour movement. Yet surely, they should not have acted en bloc without considering the merits of the issue. A strike was not a revolt.

Here, one might ask, since the Anglo-Indian did not join a union, how did he get his grievances redressed or did he have any grievances at all?

Of course, he had. With his pro-management stance taken for granted, he was often superseded by others having more nuisance value, especially after Independence when individual cases were sponsored by politician godfathers.

The apolitical, union-less Anglo-Indian preferred to settle his grievances with the management in the "let's have it out, man to man" Anglo-Indian way. Pushed to the brink, he would accost, confront, even "call out" the boss, telling him his fortune in the most colourful terms, just stopping short of 'pulling off' at him. Some bosses understood and glossed over such errant behaviour, calling it "letting off steam". A few others, strict disciplinarians with lower tolerance levels, were quick to slap a charge of insubordination on him. The lenient boss knew that after allowing sufficient cooling down time, the AI subordinate would once again respond to his orders with a "Yes, Sir, very well, Sir!" For the AI employee taking such matters to the union was effeminate. It was not the Anglo-Indian way.

Of course, he could always turn to Frank Anthony, MP and champion of the Community for many years. But this was possible only after exhausting the "proper channel" procedure which was time consuming.

By the time the petition reached Frank Anthony, it was a case of delayed justice tantamount to denied justice. With his brilliance, tenacity and clout, Frank Anthony "won" many cases, yet at times the AI victim was faced with an irreversible fait accompli which he had to grin and bear. Frank Anthony himself said that the proper channel was usually the waste paper basket.

I was just a second year apprentice when the All India Railway strike of 1960 was called. I forget what the demands were, but the workforce seemed to be well organised and there was more than a semblance of unity. I was one of a hundred and fifty odd Jamalpur apprentices, deputed as volunteers all over the Eastern Railway. Reporting to the Eastern Railway HQ at Fairlie Place, Calcutta, we were asked to opt for the railway division of our choice. We, a group of five Anglo-Indians, were indifferent (any place would do), but finally opted for Howrah.

Illustration: Harry MacLure

Discounting discouraging reports of an aggressive pre-strike build up with threats of violence, we decided Howrah was the best place for us. Strike or no strike, we could go to Calcutta every evening to see the latest English movies at the Metro, Globe and Lighthouse and feast on the succulent "Kati Kebabs" of Nizam's. So the five of us, Errol Dundon, Terence Joseph, Roy Dias, Randolph Baker, and me, were happy to be assigned the "hottest spot", Howrah Loco shed in Bamangachi, a busy railway yard which turned out locomotives for all passenger, mail and express trains leaving Howrah, bound for different parts of the country. The surprise "odd man out" posted along with us was Manian, who promised to look after us by "supervising" our ration of coarse boiled rice, "aloo choka" and a watery dhal having the viscosity of rasam. A few onions and a green chilly was a bonus. You had to eat this meal "hot-hot", or else it didn't go down well, in fact tended to have the opposite effect.

The pre-strike atmosphere was indeed awesome. Howrah and Sealdah twin terminals were epicentres of the strike, in the heart of a politically conscious, belligerent, pro-labour Bengal. Strike leaders and those of supporting political parties made fiery rabble rousing speeches, threatening "fence sitting" neutral workers with dire consequences. We were housed in the large Railway Running Room at Bamangachi but ventured out to see and hear for ourselves. A few special class apprentices shared our dormitory. Blair Williams was one of them. I also remember meeting APWI Nevada (Bobby) Fosberry at a tea shop. A smart, good looking bloke, who had just assumed charge of a very responsible post, Bobby simply smiled and shrugged when we asked him how the strike was likely to develop.

Throughout the week long strike, almost every evening, the five of us, after performing voluntary day duty, would walk along the tracks to Howrah station. From there, we would take a bus or tram to Chowringhee to see our favourite movies.

The Loco Foreman, Mr. Gavin and the Head Fitter Mr. Thornton, had come to know of our evening escapades. "Be careful boys," they cautioned us. "Keep together and carry a stick with you." Errol Dundon, the tallest and strongest, was our leader and lathi bearer. Invariably, we returned late at night walking along the desolate tracks, laughing, joking, singing and reviewing the movie. This was a brave front for the fear lurking within – the fear of being outnumbered and over-powered by goonda striking elements. However, we were never accosted, never intimidated. The five of us felt like heroes, but that is another story...

* * *

I VIVIDLY REMEMBER the night of the 1960 railway strike, the tense moments before zero hour. At the stroke of midnight, the evening shift gang put down their tools. Silently, they fell in line and handed over their tools and tokens. They marched out in the same formation and when they reached the exit gate they started sloganeering. None of the graveyard shift workers came in for duty. A few loyal ones who had entered earlier, emerged from their hiding places, old wagons and stabled locomotives. Along with them we six apprentice volunteers were a makeshift skeletal workforce.

The strike was near total. The next day, there were 40-odd locomotives in the shed, mostly without pit-berths and with hardly any staff left to maintain them. Soon, orders came from the top to drop fire. Errol Dundon and Terrence Joseph, who had done a stint as steam-men in the CKP loco shed, were part of the fire-dropping operation. They rose in our esteem and earned some local appreciation as well.

The strike lasted for a week, mostly in Howrah, Sealdah, parts of Bengal, the eastern and northern regions, but only partial in the South. The railway management invoked special emergency disciplinary powers to run essential trains. Strike ring-leaders were removed from service, volunteers were appointed, some being relatives of loyal workers. The territorial army was mobilised. Consisting of different categories of railwaymen, it was used quite effectively to keep the wheels moving. Efforts were made to persuade striking employees to return to work. Some officers were reluctant or scared to be part of this persuading exercise. AME Mr. Davin was an exception. He knocked on the strikers' doors in the railway colony, convincing them to return to work, which some of them did in the shelter of his jeep. The only security Mr. Davin had was a single RPF driver-cum-guard. Mr. Davin himself was a mountain of a man, but a gentle giant in behaviour and obviously popular with his subordinates.

I must record that though the atmosphere was surcharged and vitiated, we did not actually witness any violent scenes. We did hear a bomb exploding in the shed premises. This scared a few loyal workers into joining their striking brethren.

After a week, the strike was called off unconditionally, and normalcy was quickly restored. After having served our limited purpose, it was time for us to return to Jamalpur, a little ruefully of course. We would miss those evening forays for flicks and kababs.

On our way back to Calcutta, we met Mr. Sarkar. He was an ex-Jamalpur apprentice, a senior chargeman of the shed, but now a striker under suspension. Greeting us very cordially, he enquired whether we had any unpleasant experience. We assured him that we enjoyed our stay, making special mention of our evening jaunts and late-night returns. Mr. Sarkar smiled. "You ought to know," he said, "that Bagchida was one of the main leaders. He is also an ex-Jamalpur apprentice, senior to me. At a pre-strike meeting, we discussed your case. A few hardcore strikers wanted to know how they should deal with the six of you." He paused eloquently – we were all ears. "Bagchida told them, 'They are only apprentices. They have no choice but to obey orders. What can they do? Please leave them alone!'"

On hearing this, we felt a bit deflated, but grateful and proud of the strong Jamalpur bond.

Nine years later, in September 1969, as a Chargeman in Patratu diesel shed of the Eastern Railway, I witnessed a one-day All-India railway strike. The main demand was for a need-based minimum wage.

Initially, only ten percent of the workers joined the strike. I was one of the many loyal workers who reported for duty. There was police bandobast in the colony and work-spot. The small group of strikers marched in procession to the shed entry gate, as far as the security would allow them to. They were led by a firebrand trade unionist, Ramanand Sinha, carrying the union flag. He was immaculately dressed in white kurta-pyjama. The group shouted slogans, appealing to their brothers inside to come out and join them. This went on for sometime but there was no positive response to their persistent pleading slogans. Then Ramanand made a dramatic gesture. Lifting up his kurta and baring his stomach, he shouted, "*Yeh pate ka vaste karta hai. Apna pate muth maaro!*" (we are doing this for our stomachs. Don't harm your own stomachs!) At this point, feeling ashamed and guilty, a few loyal workers came out and joined the strikers who embraced them. The security forces looked on helplessly. I remained loyal along with the other three AIs, Inspector Noel Ramsbotham and Willie Young and mechanic Victor D'Souza. My younger brother Eustace, then APWI Gomoh, did not join the strike.

Years later, I was given an eye-witness account of similar emotional coercion. It happened on the Khurda Road railway platform during a wildcat strike of the running staff. The Calcutta-bound Puri Express was on green departure signals, the guard showing the green light to the driver. The driver whom I shall not name, was on the verge of retirement and so had opted not to join the strike and expose himself to disciplinary action. On this his final run, he was nominated to drive this prestigious tourist train which the administration was determined to run at any cost. The strikers were equally determined to stall the train.

A group of strikers, all running staff, had peacefully entered the station and were standing on the platform opposite the locomotive. They stood in absolute silence, apparently no cause for alarm to the security staff patrolling the platform. The train driver exchanged signals with the guard, released the brakes and blew the loud locomotive horn. What happened next was truly amazing. As if in response to the blaring horn, there was a loud chorus of "Driver Sahib!" from the striking group. The driver looked through the cab window to see his striking colleagues looking up at him, hands joined in a beseeching 'namaste'. "Driver Sahib!" they all shouted once more. Overcome with emotion, he neutralized the locomotive, got down and rushed into the welcoming arms of his colleagues.

I have mentioned these two incidences to show that while, in some cases loyal workers were physically prevented from carrying out their duties, such emotional psychological tactics were also employed with telling effect.

The All-India railway strike of 1974 is an event of historic significance. Both in the way it was organised and implemented by the striking group and in the way it was countered by stern administrative measures; it has no parallel in Indian railway history. It took place in the thick of the JP movement, a political game changer which led to the declaration of the Emergency a year later. Viewed through the prism of hindsight, perhaps the strike was politically motivated. But for me, a 34-year-old senior supervisor, it wasn't such a complex issue. There were long-standing genuine grievances and the demands of payment of bonus, parity of wages, equal pay for equal work, were reasonable. The time for pressing such demands seemed ripe. For the first time in railway history the workers were united and well-organised. All the categorical associations bar one and the unions had come together to support a common charter of demands. Even the centrist establishment union promised covert support. The demands were given wide publicity. The decision to strike was taken after conducting a secret ballot. I was the President of the Technical Supervisors Association which had decided to join the strike. I didn't buy the argument that striking was unlawful. In retrospect, perhaps I was more than a little naïve to believe that for these reasons alone the strike was bound to succeed.

I recall now the advice of a friendly railway officer before the strike: "Unity, organisation and co-ordination are not enough for a strike to succeed. You need something more than that. Where are the funds to sustain the strike? What is the bank balance of the unions? Do they have a buffer stock of rations? The workers are joining with great expectations, expecting a quick resolution. The management knows your weakness. There will be swift, harsh punitive action. If you were really so strong, your demands would have been conceded by now. This strike is bound to fail." Sound advice from an officer I respected but I was idealistic enough to reject it. To me success could never be guaranteed or foretold. Yes, failure was a remote possibility, so what? It was the justness of the cause that mattered. Even now, 39 years later, I still feel that there was nothing wrong with striking per se, but it wasn't absolutely right either.

There was one categorical association, the LRSA (Loco Running Staff Association), which was playing hard to get. Its members were the train drivers and assistant drivers, the prime wheelmovers who believed they had direct striking power. They had tasted instant success through wildcat strikes paralyzing train movement. Joining a general strike would obscure and compromise their importance, exposing them to disciplinary action and victimisation.

I remember the final meeting of the coordination committee with George Fernandes in the Chair. All categories of staff were represented, Gangmen, Supervisors, Loco-running staff, Guards, Civil Engineering and Signaling staff, Commercial, Mechanical, etc., only the Medical and Health staff were exempted.

The chairman came quickly to the point of contention. "All the unions and categorical associations have consented to join the strike from the 8th of May, except one," he said. All heads turned to look at the LRSA president. He said, "It's not like that, George Sahib, but I have a question. Suppose," he said, "the guard is waving the green flag, the signal is down, won't my driver be obliged to move the train?"

"Why?" asked the chairman.

"In such a situation, my driver will have to go along." *(jaana padega).*

"Really?" said the bemused chairman. "And where will your driver go?" *(kahan jayega?).*

"To the next station, where else?" *(aur kahan?)* replied the LRSA president.

"Ganga Ram," said the chairman "*kada ho jao.*" (stand up).

A weather-beaten, red-turbaned figure rose from his seat. "He is Ganga Ram, president of the All-India Gangmen's Association," said the chairman. "They are with us. You say your driver will have to go. Okay, let him go to hell." *(Jahanoo mein jaane doh).*

The LRSA president turned pale and sat down. "We will join," he said. Some interpreted this as a threat to resort to sabotage. I felt that the chairman was pointing out the extremely unsafe consequences of driving a train on an unmaintained, unmonitored track. The humble railway gangman is a vital link in the railway safety chain.

The All-India Anglo-Indian Association, McCluskieganj Branch, sent me a message through Mr. Ronnie Miller, an inspectorial colleague stating that Mr. Frank Anthony had issued a directive to all the Anglo-Indian railwaymen, not to join the strike. My younger brother Eustace, who was a PWI in the same station, inspectors Willie Young, Ronnie Miller and fitter chargeman Victor D'Souza did not join the strike.

On 8th May 1974, along with ninety percent of supervisors and staff of diesel loco shed, Patratu, I did not report for duty. I was promptly removed from service. The Management had assumed draconian powers under Article 311, sub-clause 14 (2) of the Constitution, which permits the dismissal of an employee without holding an enquiry. So were a few others, supervisors and workmen also removed from service. Some were put in jail. The strike was total for more than a week. Our establishment had a workforce of about 500. Just a handful of staff attended, some on the verge of retirement, a few who were afraid to strike, and a few others seeking employment for their unemployed relatives.

* * *

THE '74 STRIKE was nationwide. There were strikers in every division and every railway zone. For the first time, many supervisory staff, foremen and inspectors, struck work. For the sake of accuracy, I will write of events I witnessed or heard about from reliable sources. They occurred in the Eastern and South Eastern Railway zones, in certain workshops and production units. The expansive railway yard at Moghulsarai, the nerve centre of movement for freight and passenger traffic, was paralyzed for two days. The railway administration resorted to repressive measures in order to remove the bottleneck. Families of strikers were evicted from their homes, and some womenfolk were reportedly molested by the security staff. This caused some strikers to return to duty and help to restart train movement. Work came to a standstill in railway workshops at Kharagpur, Kancharapara, Jamalpur and Lillooah. After a week or so, these units started limping back to normal as chastened strikers came back to work. They had expected the management to capitulate within a few days and concede their demands in toto. The latter however, were better prepared for a long drawn out struggle. Harsh administrative action, adverse publicity regarding the inconvenience caused to the travelling public, leaders breaking ranks, harrowing rumours, all these broke the backs and breached the unity of the striking force. Wives pleaded with their breadwinners to return to work. They decided that enough was enough.

After three weeks, the Council called off the strike unconditionally. The Charter of demands was whittled down to a single one – no victimisation. Many were already victimised, their services terminated. Some self-seeking leaders had disappeared, went underground when things got hot. Some got themselves arrested and imprisoned to claim later that they were loyal workers prevented from reporting for duty by arbitrary police action. Some were playing a dubious double role, implicating their colleagues, thereby hoping for clemency. Some submitted mercy appeals, begging for reinstatement. But not all the '74 Strike leaders could be tarred with the same brush. There were many who led from the front and gave their all for the cause. Victims of the harshest punitive action, dismissed from service, evicted from quarters, too proud to beg for succour from their colleagues or for mercy from the management, they went down fighting in extreme penury. Many died paupers, their families virtually ruined. I was out of service for eight months but my family and colleagues stood by me. I had acquired, rather unfairly the notorious reputation of a troublemaker and a disruptive element. Fortunately, better sense prevailed and I was reinstated to my former position.

I know of two Anglo-Indian brothers, the Reddens of Khurda Road, who were on opposite sides of the fence. Maurice, the elder brother was an office bearer of the Congress Union, which did not join the strike. His sibling, Neville, a proactive firebrand leader of the militant Railwaymen's Union and LRSA, was in the thick of it, courting arrest and removal from service and had to carry out a penal transfer to one of the zonal kalapanis. His children were rusticated from the local Railway school. In spite of all this, he managed to retire gracefully, in a supervisory position. John Dickson and Clarrie Culpepper, drivers based in Khurda Road, also joined the strike. John was a restraining influence on certain hot-headed elements who were planning acts of violence.

Illustration: Harry MacLure

The Anglo-Indian railwaymen of Kharagpur were in a quandary. Did they follow the tradition of not going on strike and incur the wrath of their non-AI colleagues or did they support what appeared to be a just cause? After all, the demands appeared just. Who didn't want bonus or for that matter, better working conditions? They were almost persuaded to join the strike. Then, the management played its trump card. Jossy Lovery, DME and a community stalwart, was deputed to visit the AI running staff in their quarters and convince them not to join the strike. Many of them took his advice and reported for duty averting what might have been a system paralysis like Moghulsarai. In Kharagpur workshop, the strike was near total. The few loyal workers, mostly supervisors including a few AI foremen, were stripped to the bare minimum and paraded about by their striking colleagues who were resuming duty after the strike was called off. The police had to be called in to restore order.

Warren Caszo was a supervisor in Santragachi loco shed. A loyal worker, he had a hard time during the strike and immediately after, but says this was nothing compared to the ordeal his father-in-law, Wallace Pratchett faced as Loco Foreman in Adra.

Willie Platel, a driver of Guntakal, recalls being kept in safe custody with other drivers, some AIs included, in Gooty Fort, to keep them from being influenced by the railway officers to join duty. Driver Noel "Bully" Netto of the Southern Railway tells a different tale. He defied intimidatory tactics of the strikers and squatters on the track to maintain his loyal record of service.

The '74 Strike lasted twenty days but the bitterness, bad blood and recriminations that followed in its wake, lingered for a long time. In many establishments, the strikers far outnumbered the loyal workers. In the railway colonies, the latter were ostracised, treated like social pariahs, till they apologised publically for their betrayal of the cause. Up North, the striker proudly referred to himself as *'Chedi Lal'* (discredited son) and rather demeaningly to his non-striking colleague as *'Pyare Lal'* (beloved son) of the railway administration.

Today, four decades on, the railway workers and their families still remember the great strike. Both management and workers seemed to have learnt their lessons and there is an unwritten resolve, a kind of undeclared covenant never to resort to similar action or apathy again. In the changed political scenario, militant trade unions are a thing of the past. So are insensitive managements. There are better management skills and more effective worker participation in management at all levels. Bonus is being paid, payscales are more equitable and one can safely predict that there will never be such a strike in the foreseeable future.

I was told by some concerned well-meaning colleagues that my future career could be in jeopardy. The stain of disloyalty had blemished my annual appraisals. However, the adverse remarks in my appraisals were corrected and within a few years, I was once again graded as outstanding. After forty two years of service, I have retired gracefully in the gazetted cadre.

But the mark of 'Anglo-Indian aberration' hasn't quite faded away. A few years ago, an officer I served under (he was also a Colonel in the Territorial Army) asked me, "Noel, how could a good soldier like you, go on strike?"

"It wasn't a mutiny, Sir," I replied.

"You're damn right, it wasn't!" he said and we both laughed it off.

Good Railway Soldiers

Brig. Desmond E. Hayde, MVC

It is the British gift of the Indian Railways to the Anglo-Indian community which ranks highest in their mutual affairs. Maybe this was done to keep Anglo-Indians apart both from the British themselves and also the general mass of India but it was an essential service and the community was made to feel that only they could be trusted to safe-guard it.

Anglo-Indians began to live in railway colonies all over the country and their children went to Anglo-Indian schools. If they failed to learn about Indian culture and the country's history it was because they were raised ignorant even of their own contribution to the British Empire. It was the fault of those Indians who continued to be attracted to the life-style of these exciting people yet did nothing to introduce an understanding of Indian ethos.

The reputation of the Anglo-Indian people as tolerant, good-natured, humorous yet hard-working and reliable with a sound touch of common sense grew on all. They were universally liked and silently admired. For their own part, they couldn't give a damn, they were too busy setting themselves up.

Anglo-Indians filled the locomotive, traffic and workshop cadre in what can be called the Class 2 services. Above them were officers, either 'koi hai' British or a very superior brand of Indian. Below them were porters, laskars, signalmen, lamp-lighters, attendants and so on.

The Indian Railways became not only an Anglo-Indian trust but also a community heritage. To preserve these, they had to do their job well. They took immense pride in the service and set up a level of performance that could match any military organisation in discipline and turn-out.

Station masters and guards moved with tremendous dignity, wearing their apparel in such spotlessly clean good order as to comport themselves like Admirals of fleets.

Senior engine drivers, by the time they got to that rank, could be as idiosyncratic in temperament as any good regimental colonel. Trains ran on time and engines were wiped spotlessly clean while on the run so as to make a grand entry at every big station.

Mail and express driver-guard combines were formidable and no delay to the running schedules of trains was brooked. The great arbiter in all matters was the bunch-of-fives, meaning that the fingers of one hand were rolled inwards so as to curl into the palm of the hand, the whole to form a solid fist. When delivered straight to the face, it settled all arguments.

There was once a guard of a mail train, a little chap but as tough as any big guy. With time for departure due, along came the luggage van porter to say that a huge Pathan blocked the doorway, the 'babu' couldn't lock it and was in a tizzy. The little guard went along and ordered the Pathan out, but met with refusal; so he took off his spotless white coat and handed it to the porter. The Pathan's lathi became more prominent and his posture more threatening but the little guard cut straight into him. Sundry thumping sounds later and amidst much clattering of the lathi, the Pathan was on his back on the platform. The little guard put his coat back on and the train steamed out on time.

The railways expanded and reached out to all parts of India. So did the members of the Anglo-Indian community. They prospered and grew in their new environment. Centres of Anglo-Indian activity could be found in every important town and city in the country. They probably represented the only truly all-India Indian community.

They worked hard and played hard, duty and social life were two things quite apart. Social mores were laid down by the elders and enforced by the ubiquitous bunch-of-fives. Contrary to what many people liked to believe, Anglo-Indian society was prudish about many forms of public behaviour and quite intolerant of drunkenness.

Off-duty life centred around playing fields and railway Institutes. Singing and dancing may have gone on gaily but always under the watchful eye of a Master of Ceremonies. An Institute evening always had organised party games and one-act comedies. There were sing-songs in which the entire congregation sang together.

It was this life-style that made an Anglo-Indian believe that he would never have to stand alone. His troubles were known to everyone and the community helped him solve them. Great jokes did the rounds about money-lenders being at so-and-so's door the 1st of every month, but money once loaned was never asked back. One knew that if the bloke had it, he would pay back.

Possibly the fact that almost every Anglo-Indian did his stint in the armed forces, before returning to take up a railways post, explains why an order was never questioned. Dad would often go straight back on duty within hours of having just returned on the strength of the order book delivered by a chaprasee. Not that he didn't voice his feelings to the authorities later.

He once tried to hop aboard a mail train so as to return from outstation duty in time for a hockey match. According to the rules he could only do so by passenger train. The young ticket examiner who turned him off the train not only belonged to the same place but was also a playing member of the same team. "I'd have done the same thing myself," dad admitted.

This article is really a requiem in memory of a people who no longer exist in the country of their origin and a way of life that has disappeared.

An excerpt from the book 'Blood and Steel'

About the Editor

Noel Thomas was born in Khurda Road in 1940. His father Aloysius (Alec) was a passenger guard and his mother Theresa was a homemaker. Noel is the fifth of their nine children.

He studied in the BNR Primary School at Khurda Road and later in St. Aloysius High School, Visakhapatnam. After completing a five-year apprenticeship in Jamalpur Workshop, Noel was posted as Chargeman and later Foreman in Danapur and Dhanbad Divisions of the Eastern Railway. Later, he changed his railway zone and worked in Waltair and Chakradharpur divisions of the S.E. Railway, retiring as Divisional Mechanical Engineer (Diesel), Waltair, in July 1999 after 42 years of service. In his tenure Noel has visited many railway establishments and interacted with countless number of railwaymen all over India.

Noel and his wife Sheila (née Bertram), who also hails from a railway family, have three daughters and five grandchildren. They live in Visakhapatnam and can be contacted via e-mail at: *noelthomas1708@gmail.com*

Our Contributors

Alistair Reneaux *grew up in Arakonam; he is presently a teacher in Zambia. E-mail: alister_reneaux@hotmail.com*

Barbara James, *originally from Vijayawada, now resides in Melbourne, Australia. E-mail: barbara.james304@gmail.com*

Bryan O. Peppin *is a retired professor of English, novelist and playwright based in Madras. E-mail: peppin.bryan@gmail.com*

Cheryl-Ann Shivan *is the principal at Rajiv Gandhi Arts and Science College, Pondichery, South India; she is also a writer and researcher. E-mail: shivancheryl@gmail.com*

Colleen Gantzer *and her husband* **Hugh** *are India's pioneering travel writers, photographers and makers of travel documentaries for television. Their first novel 'The Year Before Sunset' was published by Anglo-Ink in 2012. E-mail: gantzerhc@gmail.com*

Darryl Burke *of Calcutta left the Railway Service and joined the Oil and Natural Gas Commission; he retired as a Chief Engineer (Electrical) ONGC and now resides in Goa. E-mail: darrylbu@yahoo.co.in*

Denis K. Whitworth, *author of 'Lillooah Revisited' published in 2013 by Anglo-Ink, lives a retired life in the UK. E-mail: deniskjw@yahoo.co.uk*

Denise Smith *(neé Rodrigues) grew up in the Chakradharpur (CKP) railway colony; she lives in Calcutta. Phone: +91 9830503569*

Desmond E. Hayde, MVC, *author of 'Blood and Steel' published in 2013 by Anglo-Ink, was a highly decorated Brigadier in the Indian Army and hero of the Battle of Dograi; he passed away in 2013.*

Doreen Fritchley-Aranha, *grew up in Bhusawal and can be contacted at: "The Quest", Shri Krishna Nagar, Igatpuri, Nasik - 422 403, India.*

DOROTHY SHERMAN is the eldest child of Bob and Louise Shea. She was an accomplished railway school teacher, and now resides in Brisbane, Australia. Contact: +61-7-54769426, Mobile: 404285622.

EUGENE D'CRUZ is a 92-year-old retired railway driver from Gooty / Arakonam; he lives in Sydney, Australia. E-mail: eugene.r.dcruz@gmail.com

FRANCIS H. MCGAULEY, S.J., was the Parish Priest at Chakradharpur (CKP) in the late fifties; he was born in Boston, USA, and was very close with the Carroll family. He passed away in 2008.

FRANK ANTHONY was an iconic leader of the Community and celebrated orator, writer and Member of Parliament. He was elected in 1942 as the President-in-Chief of the All-India Anglo-Indian Association. He passed away in 1993.

HARRY MACLURE, editor of 'Anglos In The Wind' and publisher of Anglo-Ink, is from a railway family in Trichinopoly; he is a writer, comic-book illustrator and cartoonist based in Madras. E-mail: harrymaclure@yahoo.com

ISAAC MATHISON is a retired Mail Driver of the South Central Railway; he lives in Rajamundry. Phone: +91 8897194212.

MANOBINA DASGUPTA, author of 'Where Memories Linger', is the daughter of Ajith Kumar Gupta, former General Manager of Western Railway; she lives in Calcutta. E-mail: manobinadasgupta@yahoo.com

MARGARET DEEFHOLTS is a professional travel writer and editor residing in British Coumbia, Canada; she is the author of 'Haunting India', and her award-winning short fiction has been published across North America. E-mail: deefholt@shaw.ca

MARLENE POWELL (neé Moreira) grew up in Bitragunta; she retired as an Office Superintendent, South Central Railway. Phone: +91 8019639005.

PHILIP BOEZALT retired in Asansol from the Railway services as a Mail / Express Driver in 1979; he passed away in 2004.

PHYLLIS COPCUTT (neé Gregory) was a teacher in the BNR School at Dongargarh, India; she now lives in Australia and can be contacted at: No.1, McKie Place, Noranda, Perth - 6062, W.A., Australia.

REBECCA TAYLOR is a visual artist, painter and caricaturist; she studied fine arts at Karnataka Chitra Kala Parishath, and is the author of 'Taylor'ed for Hockey, a coffee-table book of caricatures of Karnataka Hockey Olympians. She lives in Bangalore. E-mail: becktaylor1986@gmail.com

REGINALD MAHER, *author of 'These are the Anglo-Indians', was a reputed journalist who worked with 'The Statesman' in India. He passed away in Perth, Australia, in 2001.*

ROANA COSTA *is a journalist for 'The Times of India' in Bombay.*
E-mail: roana.costa@timesgroup.com

ROYSTON EDWARDS *is from a third generation railway family; he grew up in Jolarpet, India. He now works as a train driver in Melbourne, Australia.*
E-mail: royedwards62@gmail.com

RUDY OTTER *is well-known for his humourous essays and sketches on the Anglo-Indian community and way of life. His book 'The Very Best of Rudy Otter: Anglo-Indian Funny Stories' was published by Anglo-Ink in 2014. He lives in the UK. E-mail: otterrp@yahoo.co.uk*

SHANE CALVERT *grew up in Kharagpur; he is the current Anglo-Indian MLA for the State of West Bengal. E-mail: mscalvert21@gmail.com*

SYDNEY J. ELLIS, *originally from Madurai, South India, lives in Melbourne, Australia. E-mail: lydia.kemish@calvarycare.org.au*

TREVOR ROSEMEYER *lives and works in Agra, India.*
E-mail: trevoralan2962@yahoo.com

WARREN CASZO *grew up in Rajahmundry and worked on the South Eastern Railway; he is the youngest brother of Fr. Bernard Caszo. Phone: +91 9676062593; E-mail: hcaszo@googlemail.com.*

WILLIAM PLATEL *retired as a Grade 'A' Special Driver and worked on the Rajdhani Express; he was commended and awarded several times for meritorious service. He lives in Madras, India. Phone: +91 44 24881109.*

WILLIAM VENGEANCE *retired as a Chief Ticket Inspector; he lived and worked in Chakradharpur (CKP) for many years. He now lives in Calcutta, India. Phone: +91 9874852848.*

Anglo-Ink

- Anglo-Ink is the first Anglo-Indian book publishing company in India. We aim to publish the work of established and aspiring writers from within the Community.

- Anglo-Ink's mission is to publish quality books that would look deep into various facets of the Anglo-Indian community in the past and now.

- Anglo-Ink strives to publish books – fiction and non-fiction – that pay tribute to our unique mixed-blood heritage and distinct cultural identity.

- Anglo-Ink books target all readers – Anglo-Indian as well as others – who are keen to be enlightened and entertained with literature of the Community.

It is difficult for Anglo-Indians in India and overseas to find books that authentically reflect their life experiences and culture. We at Anglo-Ink hope to preserve and showcase, without bias or stereotypes, our Community's 500-year history and acknowledge India as our motherland.